Clouds move

My journey of living openly with HIV

Derrick Fine

openly positive

First published in South Africa in 2007 by:

The Openly Positive Trust
PO Box 48263
Kommetjie 7976
Cape Town
South Africa

www.openlypositive.com

opositive@iafrica.com

© Derrick Fine 2007

Cartoons © Zapiro

No part of this book may be reproduced or transmitted in any form or by any means, electronic or mechanical, including photocopying, recording or any information storage and retrieval system, without permission in writing from the publisher. However, you are welcome to photocopy the *Lessons and questions for discussion* on pages 213–222 and the *Positive language guidelines for HIV/AIDS communication* on pages 223–229 for non-profit personal use, awareness workshops or support groups.

Design and layout: Designs4development

Cover photo: Kelly Walsh

Printing and binding: Paarl Print, Oosterland Street, Paarl, South Africa

First edition and printing: November 2007

ISBN: 978-0-620-39476-5

*In memory and tribute
to my mother Moyra and my father Azriel*

My thanks

To my life partner and spouse, Andile Gidana, for your love and for being there each step of the way.

To my Openly Positive partner, Elaine Maane, for your soulful smile and for helping to make this series happen.

To our Openly Positive co-trustees, Anne Lebethe and Andile Gidana, for coming back to help us set up The Openly Positive Trust.

To Bastienne Klein for inspiring me to write and for your research, content editing, insightful comments on the title, and creative contribution to the cover design.

To Giles Griffin for your research, dedicated language editing, assisting with marketing and our website, and your constant advice and companionship.

To Andrea Fine, Nic Fine, Josephine Fine, Johnny Fine, Avril Sacks, Nikki Schaay and Steve Andrews for your loving support and honest feedback.

To Vista Kalipa for your sharp eye and warm support.

To Jonathan Shapiro for generously sharing your inspiring cartoons.

To Matthew Walton and Peter Hathorn for your meticulous legal advice.

To Rosie Campbell and Melissa Visser for your caring design and visionary logo.

To Kelly Walsh and Rhonda Millard for producing the cover shot.

To Paul Wise for your clinical proof-reading.

To Lorraine Hirst for organising our launch, Dorria Watt for your publicity work and the National AIDS Manual (UK) for setting up our website.

To Tessa Gilbey and everyone at Stephan Phillips for helping us reach the bookshops.

To Raymond Ackerman, Anne Lebethe, Ashraf Grimwood and Masias Makhalemele for endorsing *Clouds move*.

To all my family, friends and colleagues for your encouragement and for being part of this story.

And above all, to all the brave people living with HIV and AIDS who have paved the way for me to tell my story.

Contents

Foreword by Raymond Ackerman 1
To you the reader 3
1. Opening journey 5
2. Never alone 7
3. First coming out 9
4. Losing Mom 12
5. Her legacy 15
6. Dad's journey 18
7. Delaying my test 20
8. Finding out 23
9. Towards disclosure 26
10. Cesária and the music of sharing 30
11. Support is a two-way street 33
12. Saying the words 39
13. My second closet door 43
14. Disclosing to my siblings 47
15. Out of my comfort zone 50
16. Getting there 54
17. Disclosing to my Dad 57
18. Inside out 60
19. Loving again? 64
20. Destined to be together 70
21. Loving me as I am 74

22.	Widening my circle	77
23.	Labelling the water	80
24.	Andile finds out	83
25.	How are things, boetie?	86
26.	Part of the family	91
27.	Let's launch a thousand ships!	94
28.	The birth of Openly Positive	97
29.	Balancing on the edge	101
30.	Part of the fabric?	104
31.	Time out for some sanity	109
32.	Shingles strikes	112
33.	Planning our big day	115
34.	The sledgehammer censors	118
35.	Outfits, rings and vows	122
36.	The day before	125
37.	Celebrating our love	128
38.	Water, water everywhere	133
39.	The after party	136
40.	Thulamela	138
41.	In a daze	141
42.	Very low and a little high	144
43.	Uncle Max releases me	147
44.	A heavy month of passing	151
45.	Rising from the dead	155
46.	My message in the mayhem	159

47.	Back on course	163
48.	Treatment decision time	166
49.	On a bigger stage	169
50.	A coming together time	172
51.	Losing Dad	176
52.	It's all relative	179
53.	No more wasting	183
54.	Now everyone knows	187
55.	Will you marry me?	190
56.	Partners A and B	193
57.	Very hot off the press	197
58.	A time of closing and opening	201
59.	My unfinished symphony	205

Postscript	209
Lessons and questions for discussion	213
• Stigma, denial, silence and discrimination	214
• HIV testing	215
• Safer sex	216
• Disclosing, getting support and educating others	217
• Coming out about your sexual orientation	218
• Taking antiretrovirals	219
• Visibility and participation as people living with HIV	220
• Facing the future with hope	221
Positive language guidelines for HIV/AIDS communication	223
Glossary	231
References and useful reading	237

A note to you

I use italics in my story for thoughts, ideas and advice. These are summarised at the back of the book as *Lessons and questions for discussion*. This section includes places to contact for help or more information, and you can use it together with the *Positive language guidelines* on your own, in a support group or in an awareness workshop.

Foreword

Eleanor Roosevelt described character by saying that people grow through experience if they meet life honestly and courageously. This understanding of how character is built became part of my family's personal experience through my nephew Derrick's brave approach to his sexual orientation and, in particular, his living with HIV.

We all learn through experience, but it is those unique individuals who make it their life's work to share their deep-felt personal challenges with others that help to shift our way of thinking.

As a family, we fondly remember my late sister, Moyra, who was married to the late Azriel (Issy) Fine. With other close friends, Issy helped me start Pick 'n Pay and served on our Board for many years. Because we are such a close-knit family, we all know just how difficult it was for Derrick to 'come out' and to disclose living with HIV. We applauded his honesty and self-respect.

It is only through confronting truth that we are able to face the future with confidence, respect and understanding. And it is Derrick, and people like him, who inspire us daily to do the right thing. As a corporate citizen, Pick 'n Pay believes that doing good and direct community involvement are an integral part of who we are. We were one of the first companies in South Africa to introduce free ARVs for our employees and to invest in HIV education, mentoring and treatment, together with supporting many HIV/AIDS projects around the country.

There can be few South Africans who have not been personally affected by HIV in some way. As Derrick's uncle, I have a particular and personal interest in HIV/AIDS and therefore felt no hesitation in being publicly tested for the *Sunday Times* 'Know your status: each one reach five' campaign.

But sadly, overcoming prejudice, ignorance and rejection remains the daily experience of so many South Africans. There should be no stigma associated with sexual orientation or living with HIV, nor is there room in our constitutional democracy for the discrimination that still pervades our society.

I commend the work of The Openly Positive Trust, and salute Derrick and all people living openly with HIV. These are South Africans who have the courage of their convictions, the strength of character to stand up for what is right and the willingness to share their experiences with all who care.

RAYMOND ACKERMAN, *Chairman of Pick 'n Pay*

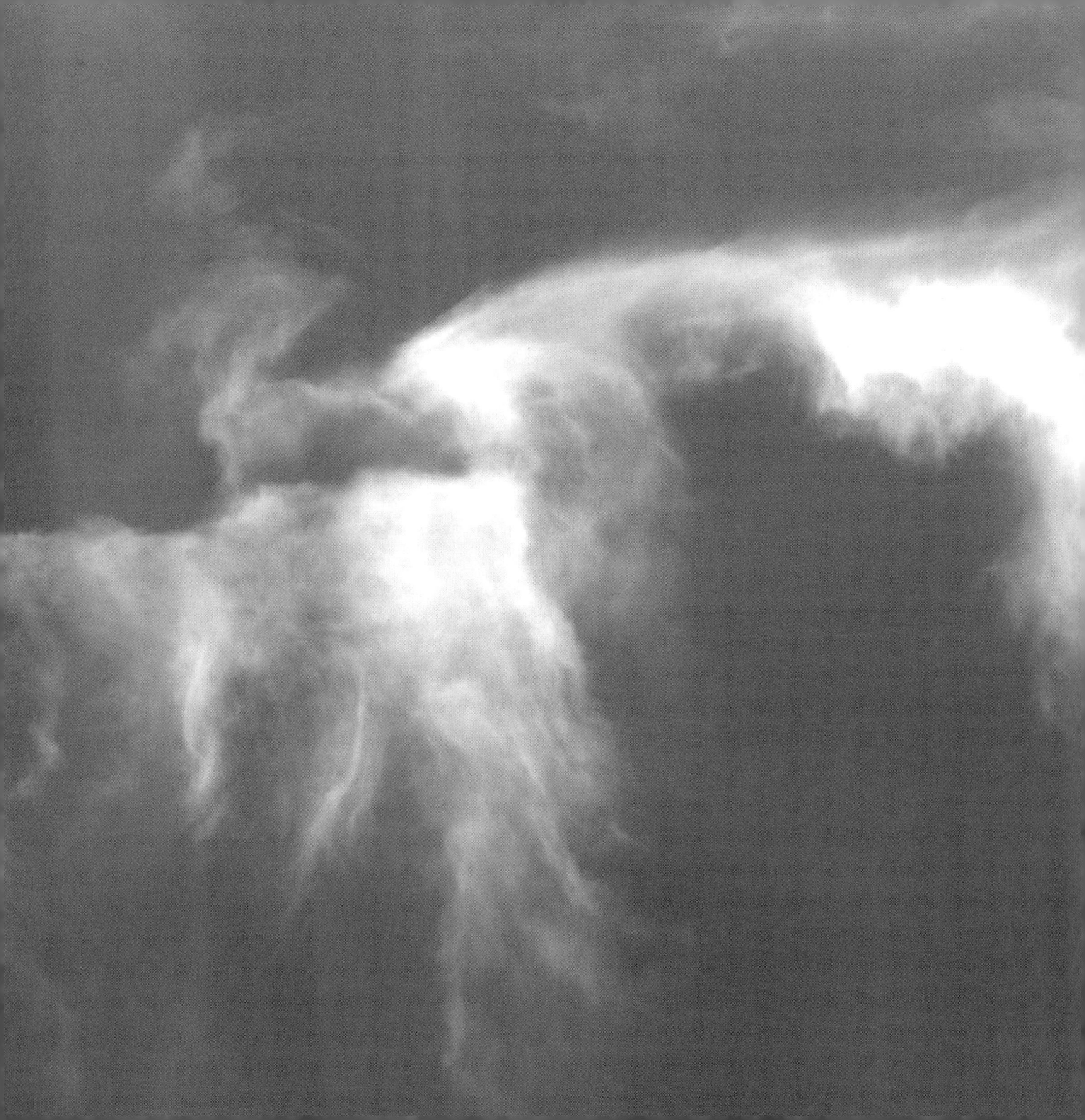

To you the reader

Clouds move. In the same way as you and I move out of the shadows into the light when we find the strength to recover from life's knocks.

This book is about moving out of the clouds into the sunshine on personal issues like our sexuality and our HIV status. I wish to encourage open talking around HIV/AIDS and the greater visibility of people living with HIV.

This book is for you, the reader.
What I have written is about me, but it's really for you.
If I am able to make your path a little easier, I will achieve something beyond my wildest dreams.

Clouds move is not just my story, but the story of many people close to me.
It's not just my story, but the story of many people living with HIV.
It's not just my story, but the story of many people affected by HIV.

This is not only my HIV story, but also the story of the different parts of my life.
I tell my story to entertain you and to guide you.
Above all, to share with you.
My experiences, my ups and downs, my mistakes and my wisdoms.
Our lessons, our spirit and our legacy as human beings.

While this book and the Openly Positive series of stories aim to reduce stigma around HIV and AIDS, I have changed some names, places and identifying features to protect privacy.

I hope that *Clouds move* inspires an Openly Positive series of other, different stories waiting to be told by voices that have not been heard.

Thanks for sharing my journey.

Hermanus house with leaning tree.

1. Opening journey

The first words, like the first steps, are the hardest, but also the sweetest.

The Hermanus wind is howling. The leaning tree is gone. In its place a clearer view. A vision of my life – where it's going to and where it has come from.

Meerlus, our family house in Hermanus on the Southern Cape coast, moves me to begin writing. The house is full of the shells of my mother Moyra and my Aunt Lucy. It's a symbol of growing up, family closeness and holidays together.

A sketch of my Mom in 1958, the year of my birth, hung for many years in Hermanus. Her picture is in Kommetjie now, an hour outside Cape Town on the coast near Cape Point, proudly adorning the bedroom wall in the place of my new beginning. A space shared with my soul mate and life partner, Andile. Tears etched our 12 December 2004 Commitment Day *ekhaya* at the sea. Tears of joy.

Yet it wasn't a 'once upon a time' fairy tale for me. Little did I know all those times sitting and breathing fresh sea air on my Kommetjie balcony that I could find love of the purest kind in my 45th year!

I want to share with you memories, echoes and chords from different parts of my life – recollections and insights that reflect patterns and common strands. This is my story. This is a story of my time. This could be your story too. With your differences and your similarities.

This is a tale about what makes us human and gives us the spirit to lift our own clouds. And all of this as beacons and lights of hope on our journey of renewed life. Of positive, open living with HIV. Of creating a new, positive language as a way of expressing who we are.

My thought for the moment:

Today is the first day of the rest of my life.

My long life, as I invite you to join me on this journey.

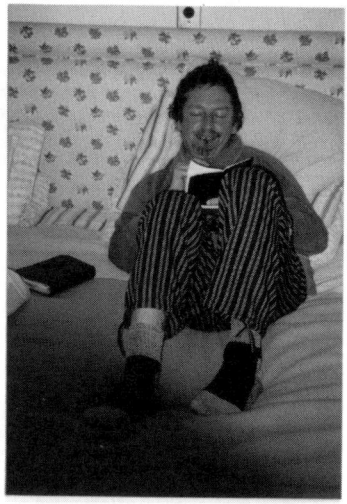

Starting to write in Hermanus.

With family and friends in Hermanus, including Andrea, Aunt Lucy, Grant, Dad, Mom, Avril and Nic – I'm popping my head between Aunt Lucy and Dad.

2. Never alone

"…No-one gets anywhere alone, although life is often lived alone."

Khadja Nin, Burundian singer

I have been waiting for so long to make this space to write. To reflect and record my own history. And to shape my own destiny, and maybe in some small way help you, empower you, encourage you to create your own space, your own new direction – alone or in a shared experience that you are comfortable with and feel safe with.

Burundian singer Khadja Nin's soothing words echo for me:

> "I know that no-one gets anywhere alone, although life is often lived alone."

Many of my childhood years were spent having to stand up for myself. At home, I was the youngest and, at a later stage, the only child after my sister and brother left home.

With the extended family in Hermanus, I was always the youngest by far. I was often picked on and, in honour of my pre-pubescent missing tooth and gap between my front teeth, was called 'Alfred E Neuman' after the *Mad* magazine character. I constantly felt a need to prove myself as a winner or 'the best' in things like playing cards, Monopoly, table soccer and beach cricket:

Did these formative years shape my determination as a fighter for various rights in years to come?

In Khadja Nin's words, I thought that I too could do it alone. But I was wrong. Over the years, I've realised that I don't want to be the lone hero any more. The joys of sharing, of communicating, of learning lessons, of inspiring each other, are so much greater.

"Anders is gewoon." ("Being different is normal", Dutch gay poster: 1986)

3. First coming out

Circles and cycles in my life. Flashbacks and many thoughts on what I could have done better. And warm and proud feelings of what I have felt and achieved.

My father Azriel (often called Issy) finds me kissing Alistair on the study floor at home to the sounds of music. Was I aged 11 or 12? Anyway – around midnight: signs of passion to come?

Years later, my Mom gently asks me an unavoidable one-on-one question on Sunday egg-and-toast night:

"Are you happy?"

Very unconvincingly I replied, "Um, er, yes." I was still staying at home and highly closeted in my early university years. Perhaps this explains the brevity of my acting career, although I was surrounded by a family of actors and managers of The Space theatre in Cape Town in the 1970s.

Coming out as gay to my sister Andrea and my brother Nic goes easily in 1984. They say they had chatted to each other about me and wondered why I hadn't spoken sooner. And especially since Andrea too is 'family' in more ways than one, as she is openly lesbian. Yet this is the time that feels comfortable for me to come out.

Coming out to my Mom is an affirming pleasure in January 1986. Wise Moyra's head is already bobbing up and down knowingly and supportively as I say:

"Mom, I've got something I've been wanting to share with you."

July 1986: London after the Wimbledon men's singles final. It's the final scene of my first coming out. The stage is set to tell my Dad. Summer in London feels cold and bold. I can't keep it in any longer. School, university and legal articles behind me, I've journeyed three or four months into my year off via Zimbabwe en route to backpacking around Europe.

Mom wants to protect Dad. She tries to persuade me not to tell him. Or at least to postpone it until I am back in South Africa six months later:

I so much wish to have an open relationship with my father and it saddens me that he doesn't know about a defining part of who I am. I want to open up our future communication. My Dad not knowing is blocking me from living my life openly and proudly without having to peep furtively over my shoulder.

Being strong-minded and determined, I push on into the known and unknown:

"Dad, I need to share with you that I'm gay and proud of it."

Perhaps not the greatest opening line, but a forerunner of my art of plain language in years to come. We talk. Dad is very much lost in his own thoughts. He cries a lot, pondering his partly expressed wondering if this means he has failed as a father.

I cry too and try to reassure him that it is about being myself, not about failure:

> *Why is difference – being different – equalled with failure? Or is it more about expectations? And unspoken dreams of grandchildren drifting off behind the clouds of London's skyline?*

It is hard, but a necessary release for me. And Dad needs time out to reflect. I am hoping he will have the support of Mom, if he will accept her comfort.

Dad retreats into a frame of mind of 'out of sight, out of mind' for the next five or so years. My then-partner, Niezhaam, never feels truly accepted. I find this very difficult to understand. We were living together before my London coming out. It's strange that my father imagines I was sharing a one and a half-roomed flat and a closeness of life with someone who is just a friend.

I continue to live my life openly as a young gay man, free to participate with vigour in lesbian/gay organisations fighting for the recognition of our rights. The movement towards constitutional recognition of the principles of equality and non-discrimination gathers momentum before and after the unbanning of the African National Congress, the Pan Africanist Congress and other organisations in 1990.

It's my *life of style*, as I affectionately call it, after the wonderful words of a *mama* from Port Elizabeth on a community radio chat show discussing children growing up and discovering their sexual orientation:

> "As parents, we should love and support the *life of style* of our gay kids."

A cosy moment with Mom.

4. Losing Mom

I make my way to a moment of destiny in my life in a state of resigned panic.

Losing Mom is the saddest moment of my life. She was a constant companion both before and after my coming out. Never judging, always listening, a graceful woman of the world.

Forever memories of adventures in Mauritius, relaxing outdoors in a *piazza* in Rome, and *bouillabaisse* and chats over lunch at La Vita restaurant in Newlands. Never missed her 16 June birthday, now Youth Day, a red-letter day in our history. Didn't matter how involved I was in meetings and rallies in my younger, more militant days. Mom always came first.

Mom had been so bravely fighting her mouth cancer for about 15 months, when she left us in August 1991. I know something is wrong when, during a one-on-one catch-up supper at the Golden Spur in mid-1990, she picks at and reluctantly nibbles her hamburger patty. It takes months and many tests to pinpoint what it is, and Mom's confirming diagnosis only comes in November 1990.

Mom adored and developed in me a love of good food, especially Japanese cuisine, but she also enjoyed just having a solid burger and chips. Monday nights are our nights in the draining months of her enduring chemo- and radiotherapy. We watch *Twin Peaks* religiously until it gets a bit weird. Soapies are increasingly her love – away from her more sophisticated world of theatre and deep meaning.

It is too late! Too many years of puffing on her beloved 'ciggies'. Supposedly not inhaling, but enough to settle in her mouth and spread too quickly by the time of her diagnosis. Mom was an intensely private person, even though she led a multi-faceted social and theatre life. Annual medical check-ups were an ordeal and seeing a doctor was very much a last resort.

It is as if she summons up all her energy for a much-awaited visit from England by Nic and his partner Becca. Mom is visibly touched by the presence of us all and some thoughtful gifts from abroad. It is Sunday 4 August. Niezhaam is there too and is very much 'there' for me in giving warm support.

Over this period, Mom rises for a few good hours in the middle of the day until her energy gently drains. She retires quietly to the comfort of her bed. She always maintained a firm resolve that she wishes to spend her remaining days at home, surrounded by a selected group of close family and friends at times that she feels she can manage.

No hospital admission for her – she wouldn't allow it. Mom resents the occasional overnighters she has to do for essential tests during her treatment. I sense and expect the worst on Monday 12 August when I get home from my ritual 'time out' jog to be greeted by an urgent message from Niezhaam:

"It's your Mom. You must please go over immediately."

I last saw Mom over Saturday lunch, and I can still taste my Aunt Edna's famed home-made coffee ice cream that Mom generously shared with me. Even though it made me feel guilty to deprive her of part of her precious liquid diet. But she didn't want more and, of course, insisted because she knew it is my favourite.

We are due to see each other for our regular Monday night date. A rising bitterness in my mouth warns me that this is not to be, as I make my way to a moment of destiny in my life, tracksuited, sweaty and in a state of resigned panic.

Mom having fun with brothers Ken and Raymond.

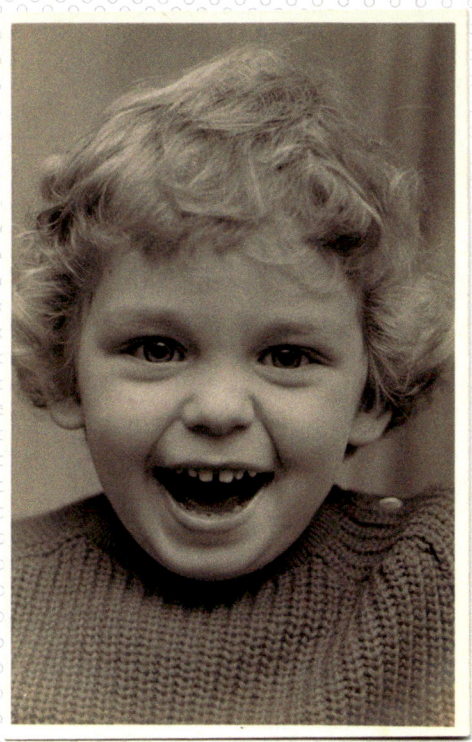
Showing off my teeth.

Baby D with sister Andrea and Mom.

With Mom, brother Nic and Dad on Hermanus beach.

With Nic and Dad: three Wynberg Boys' High head boys together.

With the family at home: Blue Haze, Bishopscourt.

An early start to the world of books.

Aunt Lucy and Mom collecting shells at Kwaaiwater, Hermanus.

Mom at her desk at The Space theatre (photo by Brian Astbury).

5. Her legacy

"To all of us who you touched, and to all of us who love you, your spirit will live on forever."

Mom passed away peacefully in her afternoon sleep. Gracefully in her space. And as we were to discover, with firm resolve and in her own time.

She had rationally decided that she no longer enjoyed a meaningful quality of life and stopped taking her medication a few days before. But we, as her dear and close family, did not know this. Perhaps she knew we would not approve or would find it too hard to accept her choice.

Proudly, Mom took control and made the last major decision of her life, telling only her doctor, who informed Dad of Mom's choice a few days after she left us. Left us only physically in a certain sense. Andrea and I compose an epitaph for Mom's grave:

> "To all of us who you touched, and to all of us who love you, your spirit will live on forever."

Our love for Mom remains everlasting. Beyond the cold comfort of spending the night while her physical body loses its warmth. Beyond sobbing through the blur of her grey, cloudy funeral on Thursday 15 August. Beyond the comfort and heartfelt messages of so many family, friends, colleagues and well-wishers from home in Cape Town and across the globe.

At Mom's funeral, her close friend and theatre colleague, Keith Grenville, pays tribute to her pioneering years in The Space theatre, The People's Space and her own Volute production company:

"Moyra Fine, as part of the management team, presented challenging and worthwhile theatre to the entire community during the years of segregated audiences in the early 1970s. At The Space, segregation was not to be tolerated – neither on stage nor in the audience…

Moyra's participation in live theatre surely stemmed from her appreciation of theatre and the ability of theatre to communicate, to affirm the human spirit and to add a dimension to human values…

A director, a cast of actors and a technical crew became her theatre family. She made it her business to get to know every person, nobody was forgotten…

The world of theatre is the poorer for Moyra's passing, but richer for her contribution and example. On behalf of the theatre family, I salute a gracious 'lady of the theatre'."

I still continue to hear our chats when I visit Mom. And place a seashell, stone or flower on her place of rest. And feel the peace of her solitude in green, tree-shaded surroundings in Pinelands at the Jewish Cemetery. Or spend a wistful moment at our Hermanus memorial bench for my Mom and my Dad's dear sister above their favourite shell-collecting spot:

> "In memory of Moyra Fine and Lucy Querido who loved to shell at Kwaaiwater."

"Are you happy?" so often floods back to me. And I answer Mom when I am able to gather my thoughts. I let her know what challenges I am facing and, in an intuitive sense, she helps me brainstorm the pathways I can take. And it's so natural to share news of travel, especially to her beloved London.

I playfully wonder and role-play how she may have responded to choices and decisions I have faced:

> *I know for sure she would be here for me in my voyage of discovery of living with HIV. A knowing look to affirm and ease disclosure out of me?*

But I'm getting ahead of myself, as I go back to the painful and yet insightful period of reflection I experienced while absorbing the reality of losing such a close parent.

Listening to Dad speaking at our commitment ceremony, together with Paul and Andile.

6. Dad's journey

Our lives can be journeys of lifelong learning.

Dad came around. He needed time, and his own reserves of wisdom, generosity and *perspicacity* (one of his favourite words, although sometimes it came out differently).

In time, he finds himself again and a fresh chapter of life in a new relationship and marriage. With the encouragement of his new partner, Josephine, he grows visibly more accepting of us, his different and gently deviant offspring.

And a natural, unspoken exchange of understanding happens – while Dad grows to be more tolerant and accepting of who I am, we need time to accept his new relationship and the integration of a new extended family, including Josephine's three children.

Dad's presence, with all our South African close friends and family, and his warm words of acceptance, bless Andile and me on our Commitment Day in 2004 with a special poignancy:

"Everybody knows all human beings on this earth are different. We speak different languages. We have different pigmentations. We have different cultures. This is obvious to all of us.

What I didn't know in my younger years was that this difference carries on very much further in life. I've learnt in my mature years that love and sexual, private life can be completely different. And I now accept that in the fullest terms.

Therefore, Derrick I can stand before you with honesty on this special day of yours. I wish to bless you and Andile. Have dignity in life. Have dignity in love. Look after each other. I wish you both great health and happiness on this wonderful day. Josephine joins me in this blessing to you."

At the age of 83, Dad is embracing and accepting of who we are. I am overwhelmed:

Our lives can be journeys of lifelong learning – if we open ourselves up to learning and love!

7. Delaying my test

Why did it take me so long to have an HIV test?

Was it fear? Was it stigma? Was it not yet my time? Why did it take me so long to have an HIV test and to find out my HIV status?

Was there maybe a flashback to my early experience of stigma and discrimination when I was 20? This was when I lived with disability for a year or so after a compression fracture of my spine as a passenger in a road accident during my student days. There I was, a somewhat wide-eyed Secretary of the University of Cape Town (UCT) Students' Representative Council, in a loaded kombi on our way to a seminar at Lesotho's Roma University. Or so we thought.

I can see it clearly now. Tumbling and turning on a dust road… concussed… bed-ridden at the Universitas Hospital. On release, I'm sitting in a wheelchair at Bloemfontein airport. An old school colleague sees me, but avoids talking to me. He can't deal with interacting with me in my current condition. He doesn't know what to say. I feel abandoned.

Dealing with my damaged back put me in touch with my own mortality. Maybe it is this that is also coming back to me. I receive my HIV positive diagnosis on Saturday 10 December 1999. Ironically, International Human Rights Day – an odd coincidence since a meaningful part of my consultancy work since 1995 involved HIV/AIDS education work.

So I was actively working in the field around HIV/AIDS issues at a professional level before I knew that they were to touch me so closely:

Of course I'd been touched by HIV before, but it's not quite the same as living it yourself. Knowing inside – this is about me, my life and my future survival.

Just over a year before, my then-partner, Thulani, receives his life-changing news, hearing on 25 November 1998 that he is living with HIV in our mutual doctor Johnny's consulting rooms. Thulani consented to an HIV test after experiencing a string of minor setbacks and infections. He takes the news almost too calmly, blurred perhaps by the fact that he is also living with depression and a congenital heart condition.

For me it is another wake-up call towards the inevitability of knowing my HIV status for sure. I was dealing with so much in a troubled relationship, even before HIV came onto the scene. It means reverting to consistent protected lovemaking and I start taking an immune-boosting tablet as a precaution.

Blasts from my past:

Have I been too trusting too quickly in my relationships? I am troubled by my younger indiscretions – way before it was fashionable to always use condoms.

Things are happening too fast. Thulani's news hits us in the week after my 40th birthday celebrations and four days before departing on an overseas holiday to try and be romantic in Venice. All this while our little world crumbles around us.

On the eve of our departure, more bad news. My long-time friend and gay rights struggle comrade, Simon Tseko Nkoli, was gravely ill. Simon had been living with HIV and AIDS for a number of years. But he never had access to the treatment he needed to save his life. And the medication he received was too late and unable to reverse his progression to various AIDS-related illnesses.

We painfully hear news of Simon passing away in Johannesburg a day after we leave South Africa. Drifting along Venetian canals in a gloomy European winter, I am feeling so drained, so angry and so sad at being unable to physically attend his funeral across the miles.

My spirit mourns, yet continues to savour Simon's life as a pioneering role model, who helped set up the Township AIDS Project in Soweto. And paved the way to open living and powerful lobbying for people living with and affected by HIV and AIDS.

I remember, too, Simon's mischievous sense of humour. It is the bad old days of the late-1980s. I am up in Joburg staying at Simon's Hillbrow flat to give him support during the Delmas Treason Trial. He is one of the accused out on bail. Together we travel up to the Pretoria Supreme Court with his fellow trialists.

It is early morning. The first of repeated calls from Simon's then-lover to check on him. No, not his health or anything like that – but to find out if we had slept together. Simon tells him that we've shared a bed. He nearly flips with jealousy. This is true, but nothing intimate has happened.

Simon and I have a relationship purely as gay friends and comrades, but his lover thinks otherwise, probably wondering: how can two bent boys sleep in the same bed with such innocence? Simon and I have a good laugh – and are naughtily tempted to make panting noises in the background to make his lover even more jealous!

Knowing Thulani's HIV status and losing Simon have propelled me towards finding out my HIV status. There's no more time to delay.

Picking bananas and waiting for a call?

8. Finding out

There is a real sense that I had known already, inside myself.

It's 10 December 1999. I'm celebrating International Human Rights Day on top of a ladder, picking bananas from our lush banana tree at home in Gardens, Cape Town. Nunu, our little grey cat with a white bowtie, hovers mischievously at the bottom of the ladder as my lookout.

The phone rings. Thulani answers and calls out that it is Johnny. My heart sinks – I did not expect my HIV test results until Monday. Am I about to be brought down a rung or two?

"Hi Johnny."

"Deks, not good news, my boy. Your test came back positive. Come and see me on Monday."

Silence. Reality. Confirmation of my inner fears and doubts:

There is a real sense that I had known already, inside myself. But yet the way I hear is unexpected – I certainly do not expect to be told on the phone! Surely my doctor, although no HIV/AIDS specialist, should know this. The fact that I am aware and active in the field is irrelevant.

Yet I have to deal with the reality – at this stage, largely drawing on my own shaken resources. Thulani gives me a muted hug, but little more, as he is so wrapped up with coping, and not coping, with his own world.

Monday arrives, and I talk in-depth with Johnny about options and the road ahead. My CD4 count, indicating the strength of my immune system, is solid at 586. But my viral load, showing the volume of HIV in my blood, is very high at 381 440.

'Hit hard, hit early' is the medical wisdom of that time. In other words, if you can afford antiretrovirals (ARVs) at superprofit prices for the drug companies, get on treatment as soon as possible to ensure your survival. In my shell-shocked state, I do this, while trying to give myself the time I need to come to terms with the fact that I am indeed *living* with HIV:

I am living, not dying, with a scary yet increasingly manageable condition for those privileged to have access to treatment. With access to treatment, it is no longer inevitable that HIV will progress to AIDS.

This is a time of not knowing my left from my right. And yet this is strangely normal for me, as I'd always been a little different in yet another sense. I do some things with my left hand, some with my right and some with either hand:

Maybe a little of this balance in my life would help.

I begin the awkward habit of swallowing 10 tablets at three different times of the day: two 3TCs, two AZTs and six Crixivan. The Crixivan has to be taken at eight-hourly intervals and it's the afternoon one that is the hardest to remember.

Apart from initial hiccups, and intermittent side effects like bitterness in the mouth, dry lips and occasional flaky skin or small rashes, I tolerate my ARVs well. And they are working – my CD4 count is stable and my viral load drops to 'undetectable' (below 50). The 'undetectable' doesn't mean HIV has vanished from within me, but it is too low to be picked up by the normal viral load test.

In these inward-looking times, I find some refuge and solace in listening to music and playing my Ghanaian *djembe* drum. I sometimes dream of reviving a musical career that was cut short in my junior school years when my piano teacher tapped me on the shoulder one day and asked:

"Isn't it time for you to try another musical instrument?"

Now, what I really need is to allow myself some support and not to carry the heavy weight of living with HIV almost alone. I ask myself:

Why can't I draw on the support I need? I spent many years from the late 1970s to the late 1980s working in South Africa's detainee support movement. I learnt so much about serving others from the inspiring example of our late Minister of Justice, Dullah Omar, in his days as an advocate championing the rights of detainees and political prisoners.

Following Dullah's lead, I helped to support many detainees, prisoners and their loved ones with advice, visits, counselling, comfort and transport. Why does it seem I'm better at giving support than receiving it?

It's becoming so clear to me: to receive support around living with HIV, I will need to open up to others. To understand this is one thing – to do something about it is the real test.

Standard 2 at Wynberg Boys' Junior – I'm the dreamy one in the second row, third from left.

9. Towards disclosure

Why can't I find my voice now?

My relationship with Thulani comes to an end in September 2000. I need to find myself again: my individuality, my happiness. Enough of giving and not receiving love. It's time to seek support in the way that I long for and need.

I'm getting tired of semi-furtively collecting my two-monthly box full of drugs from my doctor, Johnny. Would I bump into Uncle Max, our long-retired family doctor, in St Johns Road in Sea Point where he stays, asking:

"What is it that you have in your box?"

No one else knows I'm living with HIV besides Thulani and Johnny. The fact that Johnny is also my cousin is a complicating factor, but he thankfully maintains my confidentiality until I am ready to tell my world.

What's holding me back? I don't exactly have a history of keeping my mouth shut. During my days in student politics at UCT, I was invited back to speak at a prize-giving ceremony at my school, Wynberg Boys' High, where I'd followed my Dad and brother Nic as Head Boy. It's 1980, the height of an era of community mobilisation against the repressive Government:

"Every morning at assembly, we used to say, 'Give us this day our daily bread'. Today I ask you to think about the many thousands of people not eating during the bread boycott… I have many proud memories of Wynberg, but I'm not proud of our junior prefects being asked to guard the school gates on police advice to prevent 'invasion' by students from black schools during the 1976 uprisings."

The Headmaster, Neville Blackbeard, intervenes:

"I must ask you to stop speaking politics to the boys."

Boldly, I continue:

"Mr Blackbeard has asked me to stop 'talking politics', but I think that these are everyday issues in our society that we should care about."

A few irate teachers and parents leave the hall. I continue, determined to leave the school with a message. My Dad in the front row is less than charmed.

What gave me the strength to speak out before it was politically correct to do so in a then-all-white government school? Was it something in me or the pressure of the times?

Why can't I find my voice now when I need to talk about my HIV status?

I begin to have imaginary conversations with close people I am considering disclosing to. I imagine their answers and questions, and then file them away for future, still suspended reference.

Towards the end of December 2000, my friend Dudu and I make a rare visit to the gay bar and club, Bronx, in Green Point, Cape Town. The outdoor pub is still nice, away from the smoke-filled, impossible-to-speak-above-the-music surroundings of the dance bar inside.

Paul appears, a fellow struggler from our late 1980s and early 1990s lesbian/gay rights lobbying for recognition in our new Constitution. He is down on holiday from Joburg where he has for many years been a close friend of Simon Nkoli.

Paul and I hug warmly and reconnect across a few years of lost contact. Frozen in a moment in time, we talk deeply in the most public of places – and yet it seems we are in a bubble of our own under the night skies. Paul openly and boldly discloses to me that he is living with HIV in a way that makes it feel it is a part of his whole – who he is as a human being and supporter of others, especially in his role as a minister in the gay church in Joburg.

Seeing Paul is nudging me towards the inevitable:

I am so close to disclosing to others, and to finding a way to integrate my living with HIV with who I am and the work I do. Paul's openness helps me, painstakingly, to cross the imaginary barrier I have created for myself with the help of a dose of society's stigma, fuelled by the generally negative prevailing political climate of HIV/AIDS denialism by the South African Government.

We make a date for a seaside walk on New Year's Day, 2001. It is the beginning of a much-needed ongoing chapter for me – the dawn of a gradually increasing circle of disclosure to friends and family that I feel comfortable to share with.

A long, cold but refreshing Bloubergstrand walk, sitting boldly on windswept dunes and a return stagger-cum-run against the Cape Southeaster symbolise the odds we still face. Yet my words still cannot come out. Finally this happens, to my relief, after supper together at home:

"Paul, there's something I also need to share with you."

I've broken the ice and probably removed a kilogram or two of psychological weight off my shoulders. And through this, I move a little more assuredly on to further disclosure to bring greater light into my new life.

I think of an inspiring moment with the American writer, James Baldwin, in a documentary video:

> Interviewer: "Mr Baldwin, you are poor, you are black *and* now you are gay – that must be very hard?"
>
> Baldwin replies: "No honey, it just means I've hit the jackpot."

I'm not quite in jackpot mood. But, having been through *Act 1: Coming out as gay,* I am starting to realise that the second part of my double disclosure play is only beginning. And that the road ahead will present me with big challenges and also opportunities to grow as a person.

With Basti on Fish Hoek beach.

10. Cesária and the music of sharing

"I want to share with you that I've been living with HIV…"

I'm at home reflecting on the next beacon in my voyage of discovery and release. I'm listening to my beloved musical grandmother, Cesária Évora, gentle *morna* singer from the Cape Verde islands. She soothes me like no other and inspires me in the background as I put my thoughts to paper. She's been so close and special to me since the thrill of unexpectedly seeing her live in London in November 1996.

After queuing in hope, I am lucky enough to get a press return seat five rows from the front of the Queen Elizabeth Hall. A Chinese woman is sitting next to me – she's also managed to pick up a single return ticket. We can't speak much, but we both feel Cesária's emotion and soulful pathos. Entranced and transported somewhere else in our constellation, we appreciate a special performance in awe. At an appropriate pause, she turns to me and says:

"No English, but music is world language, yes?"

Accompanying me in my thoughts is the rush of the Kommetjie sea and the driving, intermittent winter rain. Sometimes I can't distinguish the symphony of the sea, wind and rain. But it helps me recall my next, planned disclosure to my close friend, Bastienne.

I wanted to share with her so many times during my agonising first year of non-disclosure, while vaguely coping with my failing relationship with Thulani. It was Basti who always wisely suggested that I balance the happiness and the pain in the relationship:

> "If the pain, effort and trauma are constantly outweighing your happiness and pleasure, maybe you should think about whether the relationship is really worthwhile. Or it will be more damaging to you in the long-term."

Basti and I have shared various challenges in our lives in the past, so it feels natural that she should be the first of my Cape Town-based friends to disclose to. True to form, I put it off just a little longer until we are enjoying a weekend together down at our family getaway house in Hermanus in February 2001.

From the Friday night until the Sunday morning, we share and give each other space like we've always done. Shared musical language has been a special part of our human connection – and on this weekend it is almost as if it is spiritually guiding us towards my Sunday morning revelation.

Finally, I get it out of my system. There is instant relief at saying the words:

> "I'm so glad we've had this quiet space alone. I want to share with you that I've been living with HIV for just over a year now."

We cry and hug. Basti wants to know how I am coping and how I'm doing medically. No judgement. No questions-and-answers to have to defend or explain myself. Just support.

> *Why didn't I find the strength and space to share sooner? I can't explain that now – but if I could rewind, I would. But somehow at the time, this feels like the right, admittedly snail's pace, timing for me.*

> *I wish I had eased my burden earlier. I think I damaged my mental and physical health by the stress of delaying, hesitating and waiting before beginning my journey of disclosure.*

> *If you sense a supportive response from a person you are comfortable with disclosing to, I'd encourage you to begin your process of disclosure sooner than I did. Although there's a generally more accepting climate now, and better access to treatment, stigma still is alive and well. So it's a very individual, personal choice who you tell and when.*

> *My experience is that it's a gradual, ongoing process of circles of disclosure to layers of people in your life – a process, not a once-off all-or-nothing to the whole world. Take your time, do it at your own pace. Once it pops out, you can't take it back.*

Off-loading to Basti is a belated message to me about the safety of getting to the other side with companions and support by your side. It feels like we're guinea fowl crossing the road together, each looking out for the other.

Time to draw on the support of friends...

11. Support is a two-way street

I feel more whole and in touch with the friends I disclose to.

I certainly feel more whole and more in touch with the friends I choose to disclose to over the next few years.

There is almost a sense that I can't have a fully meaningful friendship with someone unless they know that I'm living with HIV. But putting it this way is too absolute, because in real life we usually open up in varying degrees to people we are comfortable with.

We sometimes choose the issues we share as a result of factors like the amount of time we have together, how often we see each other and the extent to which there is a give-and-take sharing of things happening in our lives.

I am very comfortable sharing with an old friend, Bongani, when he comes to visit. This feels like a very natural sharing in return. I remember feeling privileged a few years before when he invited me to his Triangle Project office to share with me that he is living with HIV. He also told me who he had and hadn't told at that stage of his life, which was very helpful in allowing me to understand his situation and give him the support he needed.

And so Bongani is, in his gentle way, able to acknowledge my process of disclosure and to help us talk through issues as people experiencing similar challenges and hopes. Since I disclosed to him, we have continued checking in on each other and know that we are there for each other when one of us needs to share and be listened to compassionately.

...

I am away from my home turf and tenser when disclosing to another friend, Alfred, at his place out in Worcester. We had previously made love, with condoms for protection, about six years or so before I knew I was living with HIV.

To complicate things, we had been in a situation of potential intimacy about two years before when I knew I was living with HIV, but was not ready to disclose to him. This was very hard for me – and I reacted by avoiding sexual contact that involved any possible risk of transmitting HIV. It was all very awkward at the time.

Alfred receives my disclosure, and my openness about our awkward moments, with compassion and understanding. In coming to terms with the reality of my HIV status, he says he feels encouraged not to hesitate much longer to have himself tested. Many people have the mistaken understanding that their HIV status always remains the same with the passing of time. It reminds me:

It is so important for everyone to retest, especially if we have been sexually active, and even if we have taken precautions like using a condom.

...

Dudu's response – back in the comfort of my own home – was interesting and more nuanced. I know that he is a person who is very cautious in dealing with sexual matters. So I introduce my disclosure carefully and link it to my work and to some of the difficult personal issues I've had to deal with in my previous relationship.

Dudu expresses concern, but also an unintended element of surprise:

"I didn't think this could happen to someone like you."

It's as if people from particular sectors of society or with a certain level of awareness can consider themselves immune from HIV infection. But it was necessary to talk through this kind of perception. And while at that moment I feel a bit like I am having to account for myself, and thus a little irritated, I absorb this and look beyond his well-intended response.

Dudu goes on to qualify his comment:

"Who will be there to take care of others?"

Well, I reassure him that I don't intend to depart this earth anytime soon and should still be able to support others living with HIV. But I'm realising there is a message in our discussion:

Yes, I need to be there for others, but must always remember to be more open in receiving support for myself.

From that time on though, our interpersonal communication has been more open – Dudu has shared more of his personal life than before. At a later stage, he confides in me, with relief, that he had an HIV negative test result. Funny how much easier it is to share a negative result, but I'm glad he has the trust in me to talk about it.

...

Sharing with people you go a long way back with has its own special meaning. Mary is a friend from my school days when we were together on Cape Town's Junior Town Council while I was its Mayor. She is a social worker, now living and working in Joburg. Occasionally during her visits to Cape Town, but more often on the phone, we'd kept in touch sporadically, usually having animated chats on a range of issues.

Somehow, the company or timing hadn't been 'right' for me to share my HIV status face-to-face when she had been in Cape Town over the previous couple of years.

One day I feel the need to disclose to her on the phone – something I have avoided doing before. We are in the course of a long chat, during which we are catching up and sharing some personal issues in our lives:

> *I feel it is okay to disclose to her on the phone, as I know she is sensitive and aware of many of the issues related to living with HIV.*

I feel good after the call, and we have follow-up exchanges on the phone and face-to-face that have helped us to reconnect as people at a deeper level. When in Cape Town, Mary and her husband Mark join Andile and me to watch our Commitment Day DVD.

Our connection endures, as some years later Mary and I talk freely about our feelings and give each other support when we both have to deal with losing our fathers. And we reminisce, with Mary recalling her Dad's cheerful greeting to me at a farewell when Mary's family moved to Joburg:

"How's the gay bachelor?"

"Um… I'm fine," I respond, searching for words at a time when I was unattached. A strange link, as I remember the title of the first seven-single record I bought as a youngster: *Bachelor boy* by Cliff Richard.

...

My experience with Barry was, once again, very different. We'd met in extraordinary circumstances in Upington in the late 1980s. Barry was in detention while on trial and was due to be sentenced with 25 comrades in the Upington 26 trial. I was in court as a researcher and member of the UCT Institute of Criminology team doing an extensive community survey in Upington's township, Paballelo, on community attitudes towards the trial group, to assist them in mitigation of sentence. There was the appalling possibility that some of the group could get the death sentence.

From the moment Barry's eyes met mine, we knew we were on the same wavelength – a connection he said he had not experienced before, and one I certainly never experienced in court or prison in all of my human rights law days! We develop a very special friendship, leading to Barry coming out to me by letter when he is out on bail, pending an appeal.

We resume our friendship when Barry studies and qualifies as a social worker at the University of the Western Cape once the immediate traumas of the trial are behind him. After he returns to Upington to head a youth care centre, we maintain irregular contact on the phone:

I instinctively feel that I'd like to disclose to him in person, not long distance. My inner voice tells me: he may be a bit more fragile at hearing my news.

So, some time later, when he is in Cape Town on business, Barry visits us in Kommetjie. It is lovely for him to meet Andile, who graciously gives us space to have a long walk and a catch-up. I then disclose to Barry. He thanks me for confiding in him and expresses much care and concern. We share lots of ideas around how HIV affects us personally and impacts on the work we are involved in.

I am a bit disappointed in his lack of immediate follow-up interest in how I am doing:

Is it that the increasing number of people living with HIV makes it more normal? Or were my expectations too high that a long-time close friend would make more of an effort to be in touch after my disclosure?

I realise I may have been a bit oversensitive when Barry rings on World AIDS Day the next year to say that he'd been thinking of us.

...

And then there was Funeka. She'd been through so many uphill battles herself. She had felt safe staying with Niezhaam and me about 15 years before, after the trauma of surviving being raped in Khayelitsha. She had needed to talk and a quiet space to begin her recovery to get back to being herself, and living as a proud, open lesbian not afraid to speak her mind or stand up publicly for the rights of others, including rape survivors:

Was it another example of threatened men trying to teach a woman who was different a lesson by raping her? Trying to change what was natural for her?

Funeka captures the moment in part of a poem she wrote to me:

When it was difficult for me to smile
You know how to make me smile
When I was weak you make me strong
When you change my pain you know the tune
Sport and music is our food
I will always miss my safe room upstairs.

So sharing with Funeka seems like a natural opening up in return, even though it happens a decade or so later during 2002. We'd kept in fairly regular touch, always connecting immediately when we saw each in person or chatted on the phone. Often our first point of conversation was:

"What is happening to Bafana Bafana?"

Or to her beloved Kaizer Chiefs. I can still remember us going together to watch South Africa's first soccer match in Cape Town after re-admission to world soccer. We played Cameroon at the Goodwood Showgrounds. As usual Funeka is her buoyant self. Jumping up and down with passion and indignation, as the match situation demands. The people sitting behind us don't quite share her enthusiasm.

Just as natural as she is when I tell her of my HIV journey. She makes it easy for me to off-load and wants to know if I am getting the support I need:

"Ta D, you look so well. I think of you as always strong."

'Ta D' is my name from my Legal Education Action Project (LEAP) days at UCT doing paralegal training of advice office workers and community volunteers in the rural areas of the Western, Northern and Eastern Cape:

Did I really look so strong to Funeka? My public mask? Funny how we are sometimes able to shield our inner turmoil.

A proud moment: my attorney's admission with Dad and Advocate Dullah Omar.

With Niezhaam and colleagues from the Organisation of Lesbian and Gay Activists (OLGA) in discussion with Albie Sachs on lobbying for equality under our new Constitution (OLGA News, August 1990).

Mom surveying the road ahead in the Karoo.

With Barry at a rally for the Upington trialists in my detainee support days.

A whole new world for us: Andile at sunset on our Kommetjie balcony.

A fun supper with cousin Robyn and partner Helen in London.

With the young ones from Andile's family at the beach, Port Elizabeth.

Celebrating an Arsenal cup win with nephews Jacob and Dyla[n]

Presidential spokesperson, Parks Mankahlana, is buried under a cloud of denial, silence and speculation (Zapiro, Sowetan, 2 November 2000).

12. Saying the words

HIV is no longer a badge of shame.

Living with HIV has taught me to be more humble. One of my first memories of the meaning of humility was a high school spelling competition in 1976. I was in Matric at Wynberg Boys' High and prided myself on being a language ace. Pitted against me in the final was a small, nervous Standard 6 boy. It was a unique knockout format. Questions were graded, so younger boys got proportionately easier questions.

We each got through a couple of successful spelling challenges in the final. Then I was asked to spell *diphtheria*. I stumbled, missing an 'h' and said *diptheria*. The youngster got his next one right and won! The school audience was thrilled and I was left putting on a slightly false smile acknowledging defeat.

My longer-term message was:

> *We never know everything – about the world, about those close to us or about ourselves. It's a never-ending voyage of learning and discovery.*

Living with HIV has also made me more conscious of my mortality. More sensitive to loss and to the possibility of losing people close to me – whether to HIV/AIDS-related causes, other illness or passing on naturally through age.

Lizo and I go back a long way to the mid-1980s. He was a leading light in the African Gay Association (AGA), a group of township-based gay men active in creating a safe social space for themselves, while contributing to the broader struggle for equality for people regardless of our sexual orientation. I was active in Lesbians and Gays Against Oppression (LAGO) and then in the Organisation of Lesbian and Gay Activists (OLGA), who were especially focused, together with other lesbian/gay organisations nationally, on lobbying for our rights in South Africa's new Constitution.

With the constitutional recognition battles behind us, the activities of a number of our organisations wound down and in time were effectively taken over by the National Coalition for Lesbian and Gay Equality. While Lizo and I were social friends beyond our organisational links, we didn't see much of each other from around 1992 onwards – apart from a surprise visit to see me at UCT once and occasional phone calls.

We've lost touch to such an extent that I don't invite him to my 40th birthday in 1998. I get a typically plain language note in my letterbox a month or two later:

> "Thanks for not inviting me to your birthday party."

After my relationship with Thulani ends in September 2000, I do a lot of soul-searching about friends I've lost touch with. This forms a natural part of exploring who I am thinking of disclosing to – and why and when I imagine it will be possible to do this. I get back to one of my pleasurable rituals in that year – sending handwritten Christmas cards and thoughts to friends and family, near and far – both geographically and in the sense of renewing touch.

I write to Lizo and get a bubbly phone call in return. We don't dwell on why we haven't spoken for so long and who is to blame. He invites me for Christmas lunch:

> "I want to cook for my family and a few friends. Please join us."

It's a lovely reconnection and a warm time together. Before lunch, we chat non-stop, both admiring his pin-up calendar shot of the athlete, Hezekiel Sepeng. For Lizo, any guy is fair game – any man has the potential to be bisexual or gay. And he often shares fun fantasies about imaginary conquests, letting us know how he would break down a stubborn, closeted guy's defences. Basically he thinks that anyone can be 'bent'.

Behind the mask of reconnection and excitement at seeing each other, I sense that Lizo is not well. There isn't really space in a family Christmas environment to explore this. And frankly, I am not yet ready to open up fully.

I have a heightened sense of picking up symptoms – and rightly or wrongly associating them with HIV or AIDS. Lizo's lips are very red, discoloured and dry. He has a nagging, lingering cough that he disguises as due to continuing to have the odd cigarette. I don't buy it.

When he visits me at home in February 2001, he tells me he is on treatment for TB. But sometimes things are so tough financially that he isn't able to get to the clinic for his check-ups. I help him out to ease this burden.

I cannot explain, in looking back now, why we can't bring ourselves to say the words *HIV* or *amagama amathathu (the three words)*, and *AIDS* or *amagama amane (the four words)*. We talk generally, in the sense of showing concern for each other, about "looking after ourselves" and "having regular check-ups".

For some reason, I can't deal with more at this stage:

It crosses my mind to disclose to him – and that maybe this would encourage him to open up more. I simply am not strong enough yet, having only disclosed to a couple of close friends.

I sense in Lizo a deep sense of pain, panic and loneliness when he holds me in an embrace after supper. I realise afterwards that he was reaching out in his own way. I deeply regret not responding more meaningfully.

I get the horrible call from a friend late in March: Lizo has passed away. He collapsed at home suddenly and died in an ambulance on the way to hospital. No more details.

A mutual friend, Siyabulela, and I go to the funeral service at a church in Nyanga. Ironically, the entrance area and one part of the church itself are adorned with HIV/AIDS awareness posters. But not a single word is uttered in the service to explain and contextualise Lizo's death. As I consider my isiXhosa very much developing rather than fluent, I check with Siyabulela to see if I maybe missed a veiled reference. Nothing. I feel sad, marginalised and at the same time determined to do something about this.

Lizo leaves us his legacy as a brave, open role model for other young gay people. Yet he was not able to be open about his health and the possible cause of his death. This troubles me:

Can we move beyond talking about 'a long illness' or 'a short illness' at funerals? Can we lift the clouds of silence and stigma around HIV and AIDS?

I feel it's my mission to be part of answering these questions. I want to find a way of being more open myself and to help shape the words we use around HIV and AIDS. I wish to develop a new style of positive language to get people talking more freely and acknowledging the reality within and around us:

HIV is no longer a badge of shame – it's part of our lives and we have to deal with it.

With sister Andrea and brother Nic.

13. My second closet door

Getting to the point of being strong enough to disclose to my family is so much tougher. Why?

My head is foggy today – I slept badly last night: a mix of adjusting to being back on ARVs and a full head. Somehow it feels right to have an inner fog as I sit pondering in August 2005 on why the disclosure road to my close family was so slow and delayed:

Is it about the internalised stigma of wondering what response we will get? Is it because we are infected with HIV largely through sexual transmission – thus ushering in clouds of moral judgement?

Or is it, in the situation of my family, a reflection of the privacy with which we have led much of our lives? We were never really encouraged to talk openly about personal feelings – and certainly not sexual feelings. My parents never spoke to us about sex and sexuality. I hadn't spoken to my older sister and brother, yet they had spoken to each other, with Andrea guiding Nic when he was young.

I had only begun coming out about being gay to my family in 1984 when I was 25. Now there was another closet door to open a little wider. So far in my HIV journey, I had felt comfortable sharing my HIV status with a circle of close friends, who knew that I hadn't yet taken the plunge with my father and siblings.

Echoes of my past – when I eventually feel the time is ripe, I begin with my sister and brother, just as I did when disclosing my sexual orientation. Without planning it this way, history also repeats itself – my Dad is the last of my immediate family I tell. My HIV disclosure, effectively my 'second coming out' to him, is the hardest emotional step in my HIV journey.

Maybe my late Mom's intuitiveness would have changed the order this time if she had been physically with us. Would I have told her first? Spiritually I know she has been watching over me and my disclosure path with a relaxed, approving smile.

Let me share with you how my inner circle family disclosures happened. Inside me, I know 2002 is the year I have to 'do it':

My immediate family not knowing is blocking me from sharing with other Cape Town family and family in England. I am growing more and more agitated by the thought of my Dad, sister or brother hearing through someone else and then feeling like I have not been able to confide in them.

So all these factors contribute, but in the end it is my increasingly public work profile that pushes me over the edge into knowing that I cannot delay any longer:

They need to know as close family and to be able to support me. I need to let go of a big grey cloud above me. I have increasingly been feeling that I wish to have the space in my HIV/AIDS materials development and related work to be open about myself as a person living with HIV. And to openly allow my sensitivity in dealing with my own experience to inform my writing, my sharing with and my empowering of others.

An exciting work opportunity finally presses me into action in mid-2002. Wearing my plain language consultancy hat, I've been employed by the HIV/AIDS specialist organisation, the POLICY Project, as an editor and writer to help develop an empowerment toolkit for people living with HIV and AIDS. A group of people living with HIV from various organisations around the country are going to help develop and pilot the toolkit materials through a series of workshops on topics such as disclosure, human rights and advocacy. They will be asked to share their experiences and stories, and through this to enable others to develop skills such as talking on community radio and facilitating support groups.

Here is a wonderful space for me to integrate my own personal HIV journey with my professional skills in a way that will help me grow as a person. I also want to play a part in guiding the next generation of people living with HIV, hopefully making their journeys a little easier through learning from our collective experiences.

The Greater Involvement of People Living with HIV and AIDS (GIPA) Principle is one of the guiding lights of our process, having already been implemented in a number of workplaces by project partners, the United Nations Development Programme (UNDP) and the National Department of Health. The GIPA Principle means that, as people living with HIV, we should be active participants in shaping HIV/AIDS policies, programmes and practices, informed by our experiences of living with HIV and AIDS. This approach is summed up by the slogan also used by the movement of people living with disability in South Africa:

"Nothing about us without us."

It feels like the right moment to be true to myself, and to open up to work colleagues and other people living with HIV involved in the process as workshop participants, workshop facilitators and project advisers.

It comes as an extra bonus and validation of the GIPA Principle when I disclose to project colleagues from the POLICY Project:

That's a relief – no more need for me to take my afternoon dose of ARVs in the toilet of their offices.

At last I've dropped my split personality at work – I am now free to participate openly in the toolkit process as a writer, as an editor and as a person living with HIV with my own story to tell to enrich our collective pool of wisdom. It opens the way to making wonderful, new enduring friendships with the other people living with HIV involved in the project – in a sense, over time, we become an extended family to each other, a kind of floating support group.

This makes the process we are involved in just as important as the end product toolkit we hope to develop. It is in this climate, in the very early stages of the toolkit process, that I feel ready to begin completing my own inner circle of disclosure.

A sample of the President's most trusted advisers (Zapiro, Mail & Guardian, 16 March 2000).

14. Disclosing to my siblings

Disclosing to my sister and brother lightens my load psychologically.

It's the middle of 2002. Time to tell and release the support of my sister Andrea and my brother Nic. I'm feeling a little apprehensive as I ready myself to share with Andrea at her home first:

"As you know, sis, I've been through some challenging times in my previous relationship. And you've been very supportive in helping me through that. But there's another trauma I've been dealing with and wanting to share with you for a long time."

Finally my disclosure comes out. Ands is very worried and asks lots of questions – but they are queries of care and support, a call really for more information and some reassurance:

It's so important to explain and reassure close family and other dear ones. I was not about to die. In fact, my ARV cocktail had given me a lifeline – I was being sentenced to life, not a death sentence, thanks to my privileged access to medication.

Yet with criminal neglect, our 'democratic Government', represented by President Thabo Mbeki, was still in a state of denial and giving out mixed messages about whether HIV in fact existed at all or whether it causes AIDS. Is the earth flat?

In sharing my personal struggle of coming to terms with my HIV status, I off-load some of my strong emotions about feeling very strange and sad at being able to afford ARVs that were not accessible to many thousands of South Africans desperately needing them.

People were dying every day. Why were ARVs available to people in Brazil? In Cuba? Why not South Africa with our progressive Constitution and its rights of access to health care – at least on paper? Still at that time, there were no signs on the horizon of Government commitment towards providing access to treatment and making the right of access to health care real for people in the public health sector. And this in spite of creative and powerful advocacy by the Treatment Action Campaign (TAC) and other organisations in South Africa, with the international backing of influential bodies such as UNAIDS (Joint United Nations Programme on HIV/AIDS).

It's funny that my sister and I lived in the same street in Gardens, Cape Town. Yet I was somehow unable to take those decisive steps down the road to disclose to her until this point. I think she finds my HIV disclosure hard to absorb, as it brings back memories of how we all struggled through my Mom's illness. We are talking about our own mortality.

Nic listens attentively a day or so later at his place. A little more reserved than Andrea, but carefully taking in what I am saying, and giving me thoughtful feedback and support:

It's almost as if he isn't surprised, but still a bit dazed by knowing: this is happening not out there, but to someone close and dear to him like his brother.

Andrea and Nic don't judge me for living with HIV or for delaying in telling them, although this is hard for them. I do my best to explain my convoluted state of mind:

"My delay is about me, not about you. It's not about a lack of trust in you."

I tell them who else knows and fill them in on how my work is gently prodding me towards more openness. I mention in passing my need to tell Dad because he has a right to know, but that I will do this when I feel ready. And I will tell them of my intentions.

I give Andrea and Nic permission to tell their partners – both because I feel comfortable with Nicola and Becca, and also so that they can each talk it through and get their own support.

Disclosing to my sister and brother lightens my load psychologically. It helps to strengthen me for my next big hurdle – deciding at the end of August 2002 whether or not to remain on ARVs.

Venturing into new territory… (photo by Kelly Walsh for Triangle Project's 'Know your status' and 'Life is for living' booklets, 2006).

15. Out of my comfort zone

Does it make sense to go off ARVs?

So far, I'd been one of the lucky ones. I felt in a comfort zone being on ARVs from 1999 to 2001. The price of the medicines had halved and I had tolerated my combination of 3TC, AZT and Crixivan relatively well. I was fortunate not to develop resistance to my ARVs and so was able to stay on the same drug cocktail for nearly three years.

Johnny, my first HIV doctor, has for some time been relying on the advice of another doctor, Steve, who specialises in HIV treatment and is more up to date with new developments and the needs of a wide variety of different people living with HIV. So we agree that Steve should be my HIV doctor while I continue to see Johnny for any general ailments – those that feel unrelated to a life with HIV. Yes, I sometimes forget that I do experience other ailments. I suppose everything we have is in some way connected with our health – 'doctor speak' would probably say:

"I wouldn't rule out the possibility of a link between…"

It's said lawyers speak in circles! Well, doctors can't be too far behind, especially when using bizarre Latin terms to describe the odd conditions we are able to manifest as human beings. Johnny and I often joke about the terms that fall out of his medical mouth – and, with my plain language cap, I keep him on his toes while he examines me, with a query such as:

"So what do you mean by…?"

Having a nasty bout of chicken pox at the start of 2001 is very unpleasant – and of course I make the assumption that it is all linked to my HIV-distinctive immune system:

There was a time early on in my initial ARV therapy when I remember finding it very hard to distinguish between what was a non-HIV ailment, what was HIV-related and what was a side effect of my ARVs. For example, where did suddenly flaky or reddish skin on my left elbow come from?

A strangely spreading mole on my right leg in 2001 is also scary. It turns out to be a malignant melanoma that fortunately can be surgically removed. Unlike my HIV, I do not delay in telling all close people about this. Concerned support floods in.

After consulting in-depth in mid-2002, Steve, as my new HIV doctor, tells me that I am "doing very well". My CD4 count has grown to 752 – my immune system has reconstructed itself thanks to my ARVs and looking after myself in other ways. Steve says:

> "If you walked into my consulting rooms today, and hadn't been on ARVs, I would say to you: you don't need to be on ARVs yet. Stick to a multivitamin and we'll monitor how you are doing. But it's your choice whether to go off your meds or not."

I find this non-directive approach hard. *I* had to decide! I was scared and apprehensive:

> *What if I collapse in a heap? What if my viral load rebounds, as happens when going off treatment, and I develop lots of infections and complications? Does it make sense to go off ARVs when I can afford them?*

I have so many sleepless nights agonising over the decision that I have to go onto sleeping tablets to keep my sanity. And I get addicted to them, only managing to gradually get myself off them after about three months.

In 2002, the medical wisdom suggested that people like me, who had started ARVs early and whose immune systems were relatively strong, may be advised to stop treatment. And to restart ARVs at some time in the future when we need them.

Who can I talk to facing a similar dilemma? Most of my friends are not privileged, so never face this luxury choice. They only go onto ARVs when their CD4s drop to very low counts or they become seriously ill with opportunistic infections. And then only if they are able to get onto a drug trial or are able to link up with the few pilot projects trying to provide access to treatment – to fill the gap that the Government was not taking responsibility for. Or maybe they find a willing sponsor or a group of friends to band together to cover their treatment.

With some reluctance and plenty of uncertainty, I go off my 'hit hard, hit early' era of ARVs at the end of August 2002. My daily ARVs are replaced by a bigger batch of daily vitamins and supplements like selenium.

I'm on a new path:

> *My head feels light*
> *I'm off treatment*
> *And on to what?*
> *Well, I take my vitamins*
> *My vital signs are good*
> *I think I'm in working order*
>
> *I want to share these thoughts*
> *Need to share this space*
> *Got to get a life*
> *Find myself*

The real me
Again

Cough, cough, splutter
Only kidding…

When I look back now, it seems odd that I went off treatment at a time that I was beginning to gather a growing pool of support from family and friends:

> *I don't really know how I got through my first phase of treatment with so little support. It's so important to get support when preparing for and going onto treatment.*

My Legal Education Action Project days: where I learnt my building-block training methodology.

16. Getting there

"You are a person first, a democrat second and a lawyer as such only third."

Advocate Zac Yacoob

These words of Advocate Zac Yacoob have stayed with me since I heard them at a 1980 talk to law students searching for direction as democratic lawyers of the future. His words take on a new meaning for me now as a person living with HIV seeking to use my personal experiences positively to help others develop their own ways to cope, contribute and grow as people.

Back in the second half of 2002, our toolkit pilot workshops are now going full steam ahead. They are energy-sapping, but invigorating. We all share our very different experiences of acceptance, rejection, togetherness and pain. I write down people's thoughts, feelings and quotes in my role as story-gatherer. In trying to develop useful tips and guidelines for other people living with HIV and AIDS, we have to dig deep within our souls.

I soon realise that empowering HIV/AIDS work needs a more personal *inside out* approach:

> *You are so much more useful and accessible to people if you work through issues yourself first. You can do this by drawing out lessons from your own story, and from your own experiences and mistakes, to help you guide those that travel with you or follow you so they can benefit from your wisdom.*

This sounds very obvious, yet you have to 'live it' to reach this realisation in your own head. This approach rhymes beautifully with my experience of participatory methodology and the building-block approach to teaching and learning from my LEAP days at UCT.

The hardest part is to practise what you preach or what you know in your own head in your own everyday life. My Openly Positive partner, Elaine Maane, and I are facing our own crunch times in our own lives. As a single Mom, she feels an urgent and growing need to disclose to her 11-year old son, while I know that it is only a matter of time before I disclose to my father.

I feel that early 2003 is the appropriate moment for me and so I prepare myself to tell my Dad in January – the day for my crucial unmasking is to be Sunday 19 January. Little did I know that confiding in my brother and sister, and consulting with them for advice and support about telling Dad, was about to bring me so much stress.

Nic hears me out and offers words of caution and direction. He understands my pain and my need to disclose. He helps me realise I need to find a way to do it softly with Dad.

Andrea feels strongly about me potentially rushing in like I did in 1986, with Mom trying to protect Dad from knowing about my sexual orientation. Andrea wants to protect Dad. She feels, as I am relatively well, that there is no need to disclose to Dad, as it will upset him. She makes me feel that I would be responsible if Dad's heart packs up. He has had a couple of minor angina scares over the years, but is remarkably well and active at 81, still playing tennis with his famed baseline lob.

I feel she is missing the point:

> "Dad would surely want to know what I am going through. Imagine if he heard through another family member or friend, or picked it up through my increasingly open public HIV work?"

Andrea and I have a series of discussions and an exchange of letters. I am very disappointed by her position:

> *Does she understand the load I am carrying? Maybe I am to blame for not spending more consistent time with her after disclosing to her, to give her more support and understanding of what I am living through. We are 'missing' each other – talking past each other in some way.*

A few months back, she told me, she had told a couple of her friends about my HIV status without consulting me. I knew them both, and one was a mutual friend, so this upset me – of course, I would have preferred to tell Jean myself. If only Andrea had asked me if she could tell one or two trusted friends to get the support she needed, I would probably have said yes. At least I would have felt consulted. After all, it is my HIV status, not hers. But that's putting it too bluntly:

> *We have a responsibility as people living with HIV to follow up with close people we have disclosed to and who may be feeling vulnerable. I should have done much better. As Ands conceded, this had deeply affected her and she didn't really know how to handle it.*

She had, unintentionally perhaps, upped the stakes. Ands pleads with me, "if you have to tell Dad", to do it gently and preferably in a safe environment like Dad's own space. I feel edgy. Yet I know my sister and I will get through this period of misunderstanding in our relationship.

But, right now in a more agitated state than I would have hoped, I need to focus squarely on being strong enough for opening up to my father.

Playing cards with Dad is easier than disclosing.

17. Disclosing to my Dad

"Let me reassure you that I'm doing well health-wise…"

Sunday lunch in Kommetjie, 19 January 2003. I've tried to plan it with enough time for a walk and lots of discussion after lunch, depending on how Dad feels. I know that Josephine can drive if Dad isn't feeling strong and sense that talking before we eat may be more relaxing for my heartbeat, if not for our appetites.

In an ideal world, I would tell Dad alone, as I did with my siblings. Instead, I decide that he needs to have Josephine by his side. She needs to hear my explanations and motivation, as I know they will have their own discussions – she is my father's beloved confidante, and I want to acknowledge this and allow him the immediate support he may need.

In training fashion, I had rehearsed various ways of raising my own situation after a circuitous but necessary introduction on my past and current HIV/AIDS work involvement. When inviting them, I mention that, after not connecting in-depth for some time, I am looking forward to sharing what I had been up to lately – as we have always done periodically.

The moment of truth has arrived. Even as I try to reconstruct and write about it now, my heart beats a touch faster. Dad and Josephine are seated on the couch together. I am in an odd position – one I seldom sit in – facing inward and away from the sea. I want to focus. I need to focus. I'm wearing my Mom's bracelet for good luck.

Will the words come out as I wish?

"As I've just shared, I've faced lots of challenges in my HIV/AIDS work – with my involvement over the years and with my current work. One of the things that has kept me going is the wonderful strength and bravery of the people living with HIV and AIDS that I have worked with."

More discussion, questions and dialogue. I carefully distinguish between HIV and AIDS, and give examples of people I know who have been living with HIV and AIDS for up to 20 years:

"Dad, I've been wanting to share with you for some time how this has challenged me at a very personal level. Let me reassure you that I'm doing well health-wise. But I need you to know that I too have been living with HIV for a few years since I discovered I was HIV positive at the end of 1999."

I've said the words. There is a sense of sadness, relief and empathy between us. Dad and I have a very warm, watery-eyed hug. This opens the way to more sharing and questions before, during and after lunch.

Some of the questions are awkward and feel invasive:

> But I have to be prepared to deal with these responses in opening up to dear and close ones, who all have their own perceptions and ideas around the facts and myths of life in the world of the HIV/AIDS epidemic.

I try to understand where Dad is coming from, although I wince when he says:

> "I have had a concern about your choice of partners."

If I allow the morally judgemental tone of a response like this to get to me, I will destroy the delicate balance of understanding and release that I feel – I think we all feel – after the stress of delivering my second coming out.

That night and over the next while I follow up with calls to see how Dad is coping. Thank goodness, his health holds up and I feel relieved. And proud that I've found the strength not just to tell, but to tell in a way that feels soft and true. From then onwards, Dad and I have an openness in our communication and an understanding of each other that I cannot recall us having in earlier years.

By the next day, I'm feeling a bit lighter and I want to write again to express a greater openness in my life:

Three-year journey

Dad, I told you
Brother, sister I told you too
And friends before and after
I told you also

What if I'd spoken sooner
What if I start afresh
Fitter, stronger, wiser

Join me in this release
My shoulders are lighter
My head heavier for now

Let me voyage to new waters
From the Kommetjie air
Let me take a fresh path

Thanks for listening.

View from Kommetjie house to the Hout Bay mountains.

18. Inside out

I start with my own experience of living with HIV.

Our toolkit is progressing well. Inspired by our participant group and my beautiful natural surroundings in Kommetjie, I'd suggested the title: *To the other side of the mountain – the faces and voices of people living with HIV and AIDS in South Africa.* We wish to capture a sense of motion and of forward progression. A sense of the possibility of continuing our individual and collective journeys to overcome the barriers in our lives.

Will we reach our destination? Time will tell, but the mountain image reflects my daily vision across to the Hout Bay mountains beyond Kommetjie's seaweed-etched coastline. Or my regular trips over the Ou Kaapse Weg mountain road into central Cape Town.

I think:

> *We all need to identify the hills, streams, mountains and rivers we would like to journey through to give ourselves goals and hopes as part of positive living and in our lives generally.*

I am finding creative opportunities to practise the *inside out* approach to facilitate understanding and action around issues such as voluntary counselling and testing (VCT), living with HIV and access to treatment. In other words, I start with my own experience of living with HIV.

I facilitate a couple of training modules for the Karoo Centre for Human Rights (KCHR) at a paralegal course for advice office workers in Graaff-Reinet. The first module is on developing communication skills, with a special emphasis on writing and speaking in plain, understandable language when communicating with the community and clients. I use my own experience of LEAP's legal literacy work in rural areas in the late 1980s and early 1990s to help them appreciate and practise ways of simplifying and making the law more accessible.

For the second module, the KCHR requests a focus on the *legal and human rights issues* around HIV/AIDS-related challenges in the community or workplace. Thami, the KCHR's director, and I both worked at LEAP at UCT. Thami is one of the few human rights activists from a rural area, Beaufort West, who returned to his home town to put his skills back into setting up a project, the KCHR, to assist in addressing the needs of under-resourced areas and communities.

We have a long chat about the focus of this module:

> "Thami, I think it's important for us to focus more broadly than on the legal and human rights implications of HIV/AIDS.

We need to start by looking at the social attitudes, perceptions and stigma that shape a lot of the response by communities. Our paralegals are part of and a product of their communities. And some of their ideas are also shaped by what they hear and see around them."

So I prepare a module on HIV/AIDS *social and legal issues*. We spend the whole of the first day of the training examining our own attitudes and experiences. I speak from my own experience and disclose to the group to encourage them to address issues like:

Have I thought of having an HIV test myself? Do I know people living with HIV in my community and are they able to be open about it?

When we eventually get on to the legal and human rights issues, we use role-plays of scenarios to test the sharpness of participants on legal issues, as well as social attitudes and language used, in an integrated way.

My disclosure has a visible and layered effect. Some people respond in the big group. Others find it easier to talk in smaller groups. After lunch, one person shares publicly for the very first time losing his brother to an AIDS-related illness a few years before. He thanks me for creating the space to open up to colleagues.

And there are always the informal responses, like one participant privately after the session confiding in me that he is scared to have an HIV test – but that he knows he has to, as he has discovered that his partner is cheating on him. And the unexpected way people share in return. That night, at a social braai for participants, one person shares with me marital problems she is experiencing with her husband. She feels she can open up to me and welcomes any kind of advice I can give.

•••

A special challenge in HIV awareness work is shifting the mindsets of different role-players in our social welfare, justice and health systems:

How can we sensitise people to imagine what it is like to be in our shoes as people living with HIV? And, with this sensitivity, to adapt their attitudes and responses?

Using a personal, inside out approach once more, I prepare a session on *Perceptions: Life after HIV* for a group of magistrates at a training programme on *Social context, gender-based violence and HIV/AIDS* run by the UCT Law, Race and Gender Unit. The magistrates respond positively to the story of my journey of living with HIV.

Within the HIV/AIDS context, I invite them to rethink their daily interactions, hearings, findings and judgements through questions such as:

How can I help lift the cloak of silence and stigma around HIV/AIDS? How can I treat everyone equally and with dignity? How can I promote diversity, tolerance and non-discrimination?

...

Another emerging area of work is assisting organisations, businesses and educational institutions to develop and update HIV/AIDS policies to ensure equality and non-discrimination, as well as access to testing, support, care and treatment for their members, workers or students. I quickly learn:

Don't assume knowledge. Come in at a level that reaches people who know very little. Involve people in developing, implementing and evaluating their own policies and programmes.

Everyone needs to get their own house in order first. Take the case of an organisation doing valuable HIV/AIDS awareness, research and training work. But they didn't themselves have an HIV/AIDS policy to protect staff and to put into practice many of the ideas they were helping to carry to others in their work. More evidence of the value of adopting an inside out approach.

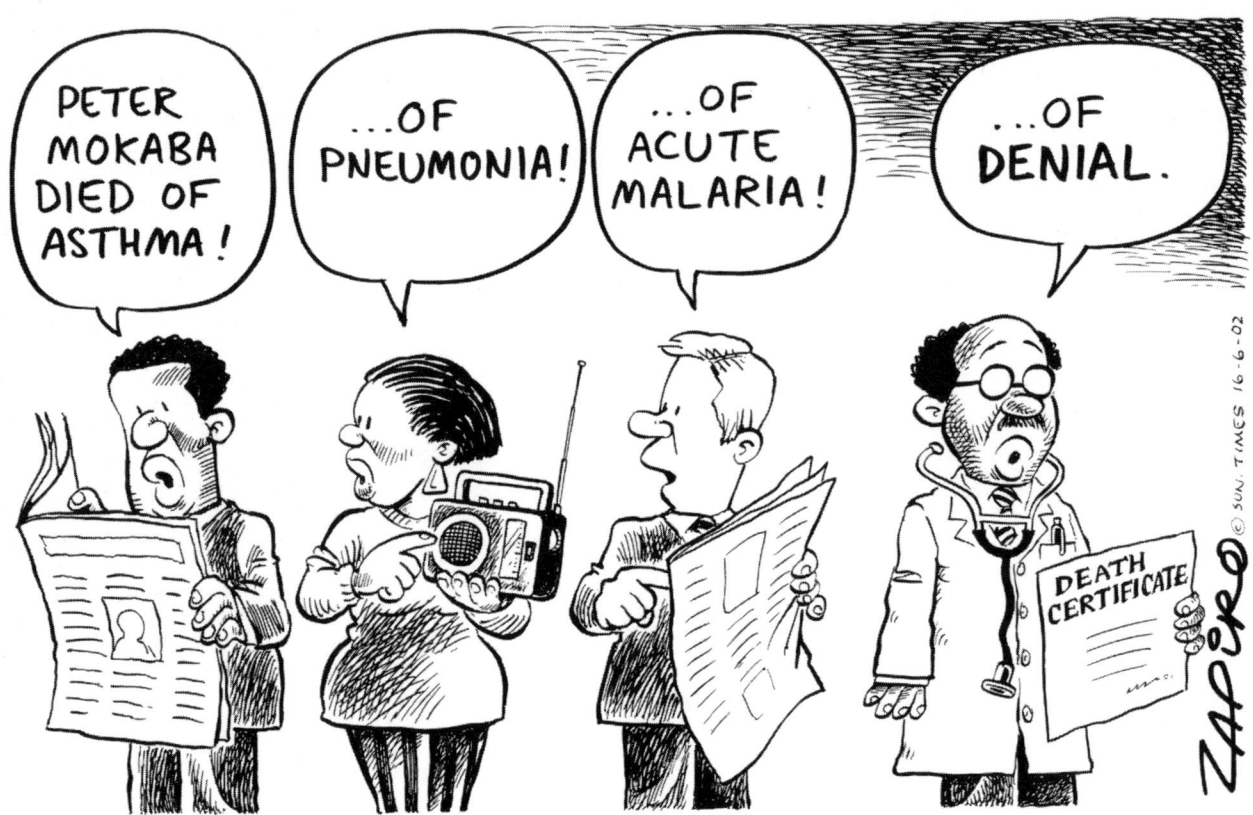

Sad irony: ANC leader Peter Mokaba publicly denied the existence of AIDS (Zapiro, Sunday Times, 16 June 2002).

19. Loving again?

Self-acceptance is the key to finding happiness.

I've been in a writing bubble for some time. I am feeling inspired to talk and write about my world. I have stories within me waiting for an outlet to express them. I have so many thoughts I haven't written down. I need to put them down on paper while they flow inside me.

Bastienne helped me find a way of harnessing ideas and themes to jog my memory when I felt ready to write. We are sitting in the Olympia Café in Kalk Bay in 2005 nibbling some biscuits and enjoying tea together. Suddenly in an inspired stretch, she grabs a handful of nearby cake packets and starts tearing them up into lots of jagged pieces with interesting shapes.

Before I can ask her if she's completely lost it, she asks me to call out thoughts on issues or themes I want to write about. She is in her element scribbling 'my second coming out' or 'kissing Alistair' in my junior school days!

"Get the idea?" she asks.

I am speechless… okay, not fully, as my inner voice has been babbling forth previously repressed or unarticulated writing pegs with gay abandon. The people from the table next door can't resist asking:

"What are you busy doing?"

Basti unashamedly responds:

"Busy deciding what we're going to write about. Like to have a go?"

Upon which they are showered with a choice selection of shredded cake packets.

I find it useful to isolate writing ideas by expressing questions I've had in my head like:

Will I be able to love again?

I was ready to begin exploring this tough question in mid-2001. At the time, I am living alone – I've been too scared and mentally drained to venture into dating or even allowing myself to be in situations that may lead to meeting someone new. The possibility of romance seems a distant dream after finding out I am living with HIV.

Still clouded by the messy ending of my previous relationship with Thulani in 2000, the last thing I feel like thinking about is a new love. Maybe it is more about crossing what feels then like an unclimbable mountain:

Who would want to be intimate with me, let alone develop a hopefully lasting relationship with someone living with HIV? It just feels too difficult and complicated.

Summoning up the strength to disclose to previous partners is also a very big challenge for me. But it has to be done and in my own time I find an appropriate way to disclose to each person – one during a long walk and one by letter.

I now realise that my slow process of disclosure helped me along the road towards full self-acceptance:

Self-acceptance is the key to finding happiness and to exploring the possibility of intimacy again. Towards coming out of my self-imposed shell and opening up to the world, not just of friends and family, but of potential personal intimacy and new sexual love.

I begin wondering if 'it' can happen ever again:

Just wondering

I am what I am
Because of who I am

I feel lonely and desolate
When I'm loveless

My HIV is part of me
And I love my life

But I need to be loved
By someone who can share

I want to give and receive
And be there for each other

I yearn to feel whole again
To be wanted and treated special
In the special way
That has shaped who I am.

Back to the real world in June 2001. My starved and lonely eyes zoom in on Marlon seated at a round dinner table. He somehow seems separate and aloof from the others seated with him. He seems lonely and at a loss, while trying to be sociable. This and his peaceful beauty make such an impression on me.

Actually, I'd seen his photo in a newspaper a year or so before. As an attorney at a university legal aid clinic, he'd taken on a disturbing high-profile case – representing Mozambican refugees who had been arrested trying to cross into South Africa. The report set out horrific details of South African police deliberately setting dogs on the refugees as a kind of punishment or form of entertainment.

So there Marlon and I were at a dinner in Pretoria for parallel conferences dealing with legal aid and paralegal issues. I am too shy to approach him. I feel I may embarrass or inadvertently 'out' him in front of his colleagues. I am at a different table, also trying to make conversation with people I barely know. He looks so mysterious:

Will he notice my subtle and occasionally darting giveaway eye contact?

No eye meets eye here. But remarkably, we do meet at Joburg airport the next day after our respective conferences end. Two other Cape Town colleagues have managed to get onto an early flight. I have been less fortunate, or have I? After checking in, I sit down and see Marlon also seated a couple of rows away, alone. Don't ask me how but I am now ready to take the plunge. After all, at worst he can ignore me and send me back into self-imposed exile:

"Hi, I'm Derrick. I saw you at the legal aid dinner last night."

His face lights up and he seems to welcome the company. We chat animatedly about our work and about the situation in Zimbabwe, as he shares that he is Zimbabwean. I am so sure he is gay 'family' and find an indirect way of confirming the obvious. I mention having had some contact with people from the Gays and Lesbians of Zimbabwe (GALZ) organisation. And one conversation leads to another.

When it is time for him to board for his earlier Durban flight, we exchange smiles and numbers. We have a kind of six-week affair on the phone, with lots of fun sharing and a real sense of getting to know each other. Eventually, he invites me to Durban for a weekend. Yes, my hopes are up:

What I dearly want is a slow romance, even though the prospects of a long-distance liaison surviving are always challenging.

I lie on my Cape Town couch for many hours on countless different days imagining how it might go when we finally have quality time together:

I am emotionally paralysed wondering how I can tell him that I am living with HIV. I already sense that he is a hypersensitive person – surely he'd want to run a million miles?

I role-play different conversations and scenarios to myself over and over. I discuss some of them with close friends to help me work through my fears and doubts. I am determined to somehow find the strength to disclose to him early – and definitely before any serious intimacy happens.

I needn't have bothered. The situation never arises. The Durban weekend is a disaster. Strangely, Marlon seems to have very little time for me.

From Friday night until Sunday morning, Marlon does his best to surround himself with friends and to take us to spaces like clubs and coffee bars that discourage any kind of one-on-one exploring. Why has he invited me up?

At my insistence, we have one brief time together on the Saturday afternoon. We talk about our previous relationships. He too has been 'burnt' – in his case by a guy who kept him dangling while playing the field. He makes it clear he is not interested in any kind of serious relationship. He wants to focus on himself. Fair enough:

But what lies behind his poorly hidden fragility? Could he just possibly be in denial about living with HIV? When I talk about my HIV/AIDS work, he seems uncomfortable and finds a way of steering us off in another direction. I choose not to press him. Our time is too short. I don't feel I have any space to disclose my HIV status to him, nor the chance to give him the opportunity to open up if he wants to.

Very sadly, my instincts seem to be right, although I cannot, to this day, know this for sure. After some sporadic phone and email contact, we lose touch, even as friends, towards the end of 2001. It is a bit like Lizo all over again. Although this time, I did not have any real opportunity to help him disclose and to come out of his possible stigma-influenced loneliness.

I feel sick in July 2005 when I read Zackie Achmat's beautifully written tribute to gay activist, Ronald Louw. Zackie laments the loss of Ronald, a law professor, who had advised and counselled many people living with HIV and AIDS. Tragically, Ronald had not had an HIV test himself until it was too late, shortly before his death from AIDS-related TB.

Three words shoot out at me. In referring to the work of the Durban Lesbian and Gay Community and Health Centre, Zackie mentions the role of a number of stalwarts, including "the late MX" (Marlon's full name). I am stunned, but deep down not totally surprised. I'm upset we'd lost touch and that I couldn't be there for him in some way. And very sad that I didn't know that he had passed away a couple of months back.

I chat to a friend working at the Durban Centre. Thami tells me that Marlon had been ill for some time. He had lost a lot of weight and had had a serious bout of pneumonia. Everyone sensed what it was, but did not know for sure. It was possible that Marlon had opened up to a few close people – again, this was guesswork.

Why, oh why, could Marlon not find a way to get the care, support and treatment he needed? I feel overwhelmed with sadness and am convinced more than ever that:

> As facilitators, advisers, educators, speakers, writers and simply as ordinary human beings living with and affected by HIV and AIDS, we have a duty to our fellow human beings to lift this veil of secrecy once and for all.

Kommetjie house at dusk – a space waiting to be shared.

20. Destined to be together

"The darker it grows, the clearer I see
All the happiness spinning
With all the signs that you dance for me
Comes a new beginning."

From *Dancing steps*, Geoffrey Oryema, Ugandan singer

A new chapter awaited me. Almost as if the beacons of light from the widening circles of my disclosure voyage were leading me into a fresh space. A space where I could find myself again. Express myself. And find one special soul to share my life everlastingly with.

A romantic dream? I thought so too. And my pressurised work and personal environments of May 2003 didn't exactly warn me of what joy was waiting for me around the corner.

The toolkit project had bubbled along. Our final workshop in Johannesburg was draining. We'd lost one of our participants, Nomangwane, in January. A proud yet shy fighter for the rights of people living with HIV and AIDS, she'd succumbed. Her immune system had been unable to fight any longer – while she had been strong mentally, she somehow was unable to pull her body through. At a certain point, it seems like she'd lost the will to fight on. The title from a beautiful poem she wrote for our disclosure workshop rained in my heart:

"The storm is not yet over."

Appropriately, it hailed during our touching memorial candlelight service for Nomangwane. If only she'd had access to the ARV medication she needed when she weakened. We would need to find our collective strength to carry on, inspired by the words of Labi Siffre's song I played at the end of the workshop:

"Something inside so strong, I know that I can make it."

On the personal front, I am a little fragile by this time. I am staying with a friend, one of the toolkit's facilitators, Jason. We've developed a supportive way of sharing our HIV challenges with each other, and are looking forward to going together to a play at the Market Theatre about the life of Simon Nkoli.

My edgy tenseness flows from a serious of stressful calls and requests for financial and emotional help from my ex, Thulani. There is an especially disturbing one that afternoon while Jason is shopping for food in Joburg. From Port Elizabeth, Thulani reports he is suicidal again. I'd been supporting him on ARVs and had agreed to do this until he was able to access free medication through government clinics and hospitals. I think to myself:

Has Thulani been adhering to his ARVs if it seems he is wavering mentally again?

Jason is busy changing the furniture in his flat, so there is no couch or spare bed.

I wonder: was Jason able to sleep that night in our shared double bed? I feel so tight and restless and hardly sleep at all. It's about not quite being able to shake off the cloud of Thulani. I'm also having some underlying concerns about where our heartfelt toolkit stories are going to.

But it's mostly about my own insecurity and inertia in the romantic division of life. I am not great company. Humble apologies to Jason and anyone else who endured me at this time!

Bubbling in the back of my mind is the advert I have read in the gay newspaper *Exit*:

> "*DESPERATE* 25 yo GBM (gay black man) would like to hear from other gays pls call … for relationship. I'm GD/LKG (good-looking) and desperate."

The *desperate* tag is very appealing. I'd never thought of labelling myself as that, even if that's what I remember feeling for much of that time. Will I have the guts to respond to the advert when I return to Cape Town? I'd never placed nor answered an advert before.

I'm pacing up and down at home again, two weeks after first seeing the ad. *Exit* is permanently folded open on that page now. I've read it over and over and slipped into training mode again, role-playing making the call. It all feels very close and scary. The mystery person has had the courage to leave his cell number – no anonymous X-box for him.

It's 16h15: Wednesday, 14 May 2003:

> "Hi, my name's Derrick, I saw your advert in *Exit* a little while ago."

A crystal clear voice responds and penetrates right through me:

> "Hello, I'm Andile."

He is on the phone at work, but this doesn't seem to matter. An open book? We have a non-stop first chat of around five minutes. It feels good. He is warm and real. We agree to meet up in Claremont on Sunday.

Out of the blue, he calls me on Thursday:

> "Just checking how you are and feeling excited about Sunday."

My heart misses a few beats. Can I still do this stuff? After all, I affectionately see myself as already navigating the twists and turns of advancing middle age. Summoning up all of my fragile courage, I suggest that we link up on Friday night instead of an agonising wait until Sunday.

We meet at what has become known as 'our garage' in Newlands. Andile walks in his cool, deliberate style across the tarmac to where I stand leaning against the car. I am dressed in my promised light blue denim jacket – otherwise, how would we recognise each other?

We shake hands for a longish time. Did we hug? Honestly, I can't remember – it is all a lovely blur. Don't think it was 'love at first sight', but I feel immediately touched. I think:

I want to explore this slowly, but definitely, yes!

We take our first real decision together. We'll go to a place we both know – Café Manhattan in Green Point, in the heart of the gay district.

"What would you like to drink?"

"Isavanna iright."

Siyavaya, as I am used to calling it. Our first drink. And then a very long, totally relaxed dinner talking the night away. There is a poignant sense of equality in the air. In more ways than one! We both take turns to share and to ask gentle questions. We seem immediately interested in each other. It is effortless. Isn't this how it is meant to be?

The first time we look at a watch it is four hours later. Seems like we have known each other a while:

Is this really our first date? Have we met in a previous life? Why didn't we meet earlier?

Neither of us can answer that. Thank heavens I plucked up the nerve to make that call. Unthinkable now for us not to have found each other.

Andile reaches across the table and holds my hand. An early confirmation of our destiny? I hope so. Like a true gentleman, I drop him at home, the room he shares with MamLu – his very, very close aunt, who is Andile's real Mom, although not his biological mother.

We have our first kiss – a goodbye in the car.

Andile and I: the joy of finding each other (photo by Kelly Walsh for Triangle Project's 'Safer, yet sexy' booklet, 2006).

21. Loving me as I am

"I love you and want to love you just the way you are."

Sunday is so beautiful. We walk along the sea at Bloubergstrand, retracing the steps Paul and I took before my first disclosure to a friend. This time there is no driving wind. Just the sound of the sea, the music of the seagulls and the melody of our voices. And our silences.

This is my moment of knowing this is it. I know this when we sit endlessly on the dunes taking turns to lean back in each other's arms. Here is the give-and-take I am yearning for. No 'what's in it for me', but rather 'I can't wait to get to know you'. We are there for each other and just want to spend as much time as we can together.

Still I feel troubled:

I will not be able to relax until Andile knows that I am living with HIV. I need to open up to him. I promise myself that I would never conceal this part of who I am. How can I deny my emerging other half this crucial information?

How to tell Andile? I settle the 'when' by inviting him to Kommetjie for the first time on Monday night. I feel a tiny bit more relaxed once I've made the decision not to delay my next moment of truth any longer:

Will he be shocked? Will he reject me? Will he maybe reveal a part of him I don't know about yet?

In organising and practising my thoughts, I develop an odd mnemonic to try to remember what it is I want to talk about when disclosing:

LP (life is a puzzle)

TNT (trust, never hurting or putting at risk, to the other side of the mountain – the toolkit)

PLOP (positive living, being open to partners).

I don't think that it came out exactly that way. But somehow resorting to this comforting tool from my school and university exams cramming days is a help.

Andile is looking at me with his naughty, knowing smile while I spin the web of introducing the HIV/AIDS and human rights work I am involved in. It's a much shorter version of the soft approach I used when disclosing to my Dad.

Andile seems a little perplexed, although he listens attentively without interrupting me. My first insight into his extraordinary patience and politeness:

"I'm sharing all these things with you to help you understand me. I'm also living with HIV and I decided I want you to know before anything intimate happens between us."

And so my baby knew. The ceiling never caved in. The Kommetjie waves continued to rush and crash.

Andile looks at me in surprise, but not the kind of surprise you may have expected:

"Why should that make any difference? I love you and want to love you just the way you are."

What an amazing response:

I want to bounce up and down. I didn't know what to expect, but I didn't expect such calmness, such maturity.

Our age gap of 19 years seems so irrelevant. His wisdom and our growing love for each other are already beginning to transcend any barriers that we may have thought could exist between us. Afterwards, we often laugh about this moment. He shares what he was thinking:

"Why is he telling this long story?"

We talk and talk. Andile had tested a number of years previously. He shares that he was HIV negative then. He tells me he now feels the need to test again, but is scared. He says he will have a fresh HIV test when he feels ready.

We know then that we will always be there for each other:

Andile begins supporting me as his partner living with HIV. And I start supporting him by helping to prepare him for testing again. We agree that we will love each other safely. What we have is much too precious.

I know that my wistful lone moments on the balcony are over. From now on my Kommetjie home, *Cesária*, is to be a shared space – a haven, our castle, a place where our souls and bodies intertwine.

We begin to appreciate and understand each other in a way that neither of us has experienced before. Our search is over. No more desperation, just devotion to each other and to building our relationship on a powerful foundation of trust and hope in a shared future.

With Ken and Joan in their Golders Green garden, London.

22. Widening my circle

The path of disclosure is truly ongoing.

I am overflowing with loving and being loved again. How will we be able to survive three weeks apart? I am off on a long-planned trip to England to visit family and friends, highlighted by a constant beacon of light in my life – the WOMAD (World of Music, Arts and Dance) festival in Reading over the last weekend of July.

Around my neck is our engagement necklace. I had bought two little cowrie shell pendants in the marketplace in Stone Town, Zanzibar, while working in Tanzania about five years before. I had waited patiently for the moment to share them with someone very special. And now we each wear one to symbolise our tight bond across the air miles.

Another strong passion is energising this visit – my need to widen my circle of disclosure to include my close English family on my Mom's side. It was always the next logical family step in my head after getting over the hurdle of disclosing to Dad.

The path of disclosure is truly ongoing – and here I am plotting my next moves as I soar into the Cape Town skies en route to London:

Who will I tell? When? How? I wish to break my news in a way that will not alarm dear family and friends abroad. Yet I want them to know what is happening to me and in this way to deepen our bonds of sharing and being there for each other.

This is so true for Aunt Joan, wife of Ken, my Mom's younger brother. Like Moyra, Joan has been bravely living with cancer for a few years. She has endured various bursts of chemo- and radiotherapy for her breast cancer. I remember how she and Ken, and all our English family, were with us in spirit when Mom was ill. We delayed Mom's funeral by a day for Uncle Ken to be with us on the day of his sister's funeral in Cape Town.

Our favourite Café Japan is closed on my disclosure night. So, after a drink in a place of much pride – Joan and Ken's cosy garden – we make our way to a lovely Chinese place not far from Golders Green. As usual, we have so much to catch up on – and because the moment doesn't feel quite right, I don't feel I have the space to share my disclosure at the house.

And as we drift our way through a very slow and relaxing dinner, it somehow feels more important for me to first find out more about how *they* are. Ken shares how he is coping with his multiple sclerosis and his gradually reduced mobility. And Joan updates me on how she is doing.

In between, nibbles, a glass or two of wine, and loads of questions about this and that. And tales of their past and planned travels. They really are a celebration of life and rarely complain about the 'ailment division'.

Hmm. How am I going to get a word in edgeways? Another gulp of wine might help:

> "How about another touch of... Now tell us about..." from Joan.

> My turn: "I've always valued both of you in your openness in sharing what's happening in your lives. How you've coped in tough times. And the interest you've shown in me."

I am crossing a bridge. Another mouthful and I'll be ready:

> "I've also been wanting to share a special health challenge that I've been facing."

And so my disclosure unfolds. I start, as usual, by assuring them that there is no need for alarm, as I am coping and doing quite well. I explain my journey since 1999 and how I am then, in 2003, off treatment and why.

There is naturally a sense of concern. But mainly just a feeling of warmth and support. And a number of questions searching for information and an understanding of our strange South African landscape of government inertia and denial on HIV/AIDS.

I share how I plan to tell other English family I will be staying with or seeing. I ask them to allow me to tell them directly myself, but add that they are most welcome to chat and share as family afterwards:

> *After all, they need to share and off-load with each other too. And I want to encourage a sense that it is very much okay for us to talk about the fact that I am living with and most certainly alive with HIV!*

I feel a deep sense of relief and peace as I take the London underground train back to King's Cross. My strong bond to my English clan is one of my close links to my Mom. So I am very glad that Ken and Joan know.

Welcoming flags at the WOMAD music festival.

23. Labelling the water

Isn't this meant to be a holiday?

Disclosure, like life, is full of unexpected twists and turns. And there I am thinking that sharing with Ken and Joan will be the tricky disclosure in England.

Telling cousins Roy and Ursula, and Robyn and Helen, had gone as well as difficult personal news can. I feel that they now better understood my world – my personal life, my love, my work – and how these have mingled into a meaningful whole.

Stepping off the train at Leicester to visit friends Tim, Ruby and family, I think that the last piece of my English family and friends jigsaw will simply drop into place. We enjoy a homely Friday night supper, with lots of catching up, thoughts for the week ahead, fun and giggling.

It feels right to wait for a late night chat with Tim and Ruby after young Natalie and Richard have gone to bed. I share, we hug, and it seems a smooth ride. I know there will be some more questions, especially from Tim. Questions of care and concern linked to an admission of "not knowing a lot about HIV". My disclosure is received very warmly, yet an unexpected follow-up twist awaits me.

"Let's play tennis!" And we did on the Saturday morning on an old court full of cracks and character. The tennis is enjoyably competitive and we take turns to partner each other. There is a feverish sense of making the best of a break in the clouds and rain of a typically English summer.

A pause in play. I'm feeling a bit thirsty from my exertions and my favourite tennis spot – the net. A spontaneous offer from Richard:

"Like some water?"

No reason not to accept his water bottle and a welcome sip. I take a gulp and return the bottle to Richard. Suddenly Tim has gone like a bolt of lightning. Off the court for a wee I suppose? He returns with extra water bottles, announcing cheerfully:

"We've got plenty of spares."

I am handed my very own bottle. A sinking feeling descends on me, but I decide not to respond then:

Isn't this meant to be a holiday? Am I being oversensitive? Surely Tim didn't go to all that trouble to avoid me sharing a water bottle with Richard again?

My doubts about the holiday joyride are confirmed on the Sunday afternoon. We go on a marathon canoe trip up a nearby river. There is hardly time to take in the wonderful surroundings and my suspect rowing technique feels under scrutiny.

A brief break in the exercise routine confirms my worst fears. Out come bottles of water – this time individually labelled with our names on:

Oh no, this is too much! How can my well-educated friend think that there is a risk of HIV transmission by sharing water?

I allow the day to pass. But I decide to engage Tim on how I am feeling that night. He takes it well and is open about his natural parental defensiveness:

"I didn't really know – but was just worried for Richard."

I am glad we can talk about it and clear the air:

I had to rise above this and realise that 'education in life' doesn't necessarily mean 'education in HIV/ AIDS' – an experience actually quite removed from the day-to-day lives of the majority in England.

At least I have my treasured music to console me – a new discovery, Manecas Costa, who I will see at WOMAD. Tales of love and life from Guinea-Bissau in West Africa. And a sense of a new 'our song' for Andile and me – *Pertu di bo (Close to you)*. It makes me cry tears of joy, tears of anxiety, tears of relief and of missing him so much.

Andile in thoughtful pose before taking decisive action.

24. Andile finds out

We know we are in this together in more ways than one.

My baby is edging towards having a fresh HIV test. We talk about it every now and then, etched against windy sunsets and the puffy, crimson Kommetjie night-sky.

It is Andile's choice to make. I am his sounding board, his closest ear when he needs to talk about it. I take care to put no pressure on him – my slow, hesitant journey to testing is all too fresh in my memory. I just want to be there for him and give him a supportive environment to go for it when he feels ready. As he was there when I needed to off-load about living with HIV.

We had decided together to protect ourselves and our precious love by taking safer sex precautions – at least until we each know our current HIV status and maybe forever:

> *It's so important and nice to talk openly about these things as partners. So easy to get carried away by spontaneity and moments of pleasure. So much harder to think about not infecting each other, the risks of re-infection, or the possibility of getting a different HIV strain that may be resistant to certain medication.*

Andile bravely decides he is ready to know in October 2003. So much more courage than me when I put off knowing officially until my destiny in 1999! It feels right for him. And I, too, will feel more comfortable knowing his current HIV status.

We are so settled now. We've been living together in Kommetjie for almost three months. This is our space. Our lives. Looking back, it feels like we needed to know to plan and preserve our joint future as a couple.

When 4 November dawns, we journey through to our HIV doctor Steve in Rondebosch:

> "Andile, your results have come back. And they are positive. I know that's hectic news to get, so let's talk about it."

Yes, Andile was scared to know the truth. As with me, it felt like a probable truth, a likely truth. He takes it boldly – kind of how he seems to take every day: 'this is the first day of the rest of my life and I'm going to give it my best shot'.

Now, his maturity echoes his worldly acceptance of my HIV status six months before. We clasp hands – his right and my left meet in an embrace of a shared existence, now strengthened in a way I would still not have wished on anyone.

We hug. We know we are in this together in more ways than one. Steve provides commentary, in typically upfront style:

"But your CD4 count is looking very good and you have Derrick's support to deal with this as a couple."

A fresh air lunch seems best for our slightly heavy heads. We sit outdoors pondering over green salads at Rhodes Memorial. An unplanned connection near where we stopped for a late night cuddle and quiet moment when we were dating and my virginal (well, almost) partner-in-waiting had to be dropped off in case he changed into Cinderella's pumpkin at midnight.

I let Andile talk and share his feelings, his doubts and his recollections of naughty liaisons before we met. We have moments of pregnant silence too. It feels so good to be a shoulder for this precious soul that I love so dearly:

The fresh feta and rocket make us even more determined to look after each other. To make sure we live positively and purposefully. And in a way that we nurture living with HIV as one unchangeable part of our everyday being. Hopefully, after the initial dawn of knowing, this will not overwhelm us, but rather inform our relationship and our connections with others with a positive, meaningful spirit.

We will handle this as a team. We decide to begin a new institution – taking blood tests together every six months, followed by joint medical appointments with Steve.

With Venetia at work at the Institute of Criminology, University of Cape Town.

25. How are things, boetie?

There is no need to dress up my disclosure in long introductions…

Venetia was a very dear friend dating back to the early 1980s when I was a law student doing a final-year course at the Institute of Criminology, UCT. This is the place I would return to from 1987 to 1994 while employed in the LEAP paralegal training project. She was a legendary administrator, receptionist and office manager over many years.

Venetia was truly larger than life. She made an immediate impression on me. A lasting friendship began that blossomed when I worked for LEAP and we were in daily contact with each other.

She struggled through lots of health challenges in her life, including epilepsy, asthma and emphysema. Venische, as I called her, always shared and very rarely complained. We enjoyed so many jokes and priceless telephone conversations together. She would just phone for a chat:

> "How are things, boetie? Haven't heard from you in ages. How did you go on your trip to…?"

And I would phone her for catch-up chats. I could always hear in her slightly wheezy voice if one of her ailments was in the air. At a certain point, she gave up smoking because of her breathing problems. I was more than a little miffed to hear at a later stage that she used to still have an occasional drag (or more?) with fellow smokers. She would have been too embarrassed to tell me this, as she knew I had become a passionate anti-smoker after losing my Mom to mouth cancer in 1991.

It is only a question of time for me to find the right moment to disclose to Venische as part of my inner circle period of disclosing to close friends. As her health is up and down at the time, I wait for a period when she is in a good phase before joining her at her Tamboerskloof flat with a bunch of sweet bananas from my Gardens tree.

Maradona – an old time nickname from her blue tracksuit worn during the 1990 World Cup – collapses into the comfy couch in her lounge and is, as usual, all eyes and ears. This is one of her enduring qualities – while a true chatterbox and sharer of titbits, she has an amazing ability to listen compassionately:

> *There is no need to dress up my disclosure in long introductions for Venische. I feel that she has sensed it, or at least sensed that something is not quite right, even before I disclose. In some ways, a bit like my Mom when I came out as gay.*

Venische has previously, I think even before I knew I was living with HIV, shared the pain of losing her next door neighbour in her Observatory days to AIDS after a long, mostly lonely period of illness.

So it is easy to tell her and I know she is there for me. Venische is sad, but very supportive. She asks lots of questions to make sure I am really coping and not just putting on a brave face. In time, she becomes a valuable sounding board for me when I am working through the pros and cons of telling my family.

After my life-changing move to the sea at Kommetjie in February 2002, she so much enjoys her occasional weekend sleepover visits. The sea air is so good for her and she literally gulps it in. Being a much better early morning person than I am, she would get up very early and sit quietly on the balcony enjoying the peace and openness of the surroundings.

In August 2003, we have our usual *lekker* animated lunch together at her work at UCT. We laugh:

> "The students in the canteen look so young. And look at us with our tinges of grey!"

Venische is so excited about her forthcoming trip to England – her first in 25 years to be re-acquainted with her sister and family there.

On her return, we make an October supper date at one of our favourites – Mario's in Green Point. We love their food – it is old-fashioned Italian with a homemade taste. We often have their tripe and pasta, although it can never rival Venische's own tripe or legendary *tamatiebredie*.

I am thrilled that Andile is finally meeting Venische, who he had heard so much about. We have been together since May that year, but the opportunity for a threesome supper does not arise until after Venische's historic trip.

At Mario's, she is like an excited schoolgirl sharing photos, including ones of family grandchildren, who took to her like a duck to water. There are, of course, the usual anecdotes in Venetian detail, like the verbal spat she had with a man on a bench in a park they were relaxing in. It is a lovely evening. She even takes a couple of photos to finish a spool – the first time I remember ever seeing her with a camera. But very sadly, it is the last time we will see her alive.

We speak as usual on the phone in November, including her wishes on my 17 November birthday – we never miss each other's birthday. She tells me that, at last to her relief, she is going to a private hospital to have a back operation to relieve her of long-term pain. Apparently, her doctor says the operation is safe for her in spite of her other conditions.

I phone to wish her well before she goes in. On 6 December, a mutual friend calls to give me the shocking news: Venische has gone into a coma. During the back operation, she had an asthma attack. The operation was stopped. She stabilised, but then had a relapse and struggled to breathe. This was the time, as far as I am aware, that she lapsed into a deep coma. To this day, it is not clear why the nursing staff was unable to help her sooner when she couldn't breathe.

Venische never recovered. Her local family were joined by the overseas contingent. They had to make an extremely painful decision to ask for her life-support machine to be switched off on 16 December after doctors had for days indicated that there was no hope.

I remember touching her when she was still warm earlier on while in her coma, just as I had done after losing my Mom. In Venische's case, we just hoped that her eye and body movements would signal a recovery. As a caring fighter for the rights of others, she deserved a miracle. It was not to be.

She left us at 54 – my friend, a kind of aunt to me, and now a source of irreplaceable memories. At her funeral I am honoured to be one of three close friends asked by the family to speak. I know I will be choking, so I write this poem dedicated to her:

Venische
Go in peace

You skelled
You joked

You coughed
You poked fun playfully

You listened
You skinnered naughtily

You ate lustily
Your tamatiebredie was the best

You farted
You were nicely skelm

You had a master's degree in vloeking
You invented plain language

You shared your burdens
Yet you never complained

Above all, you gave
You lit up lives around you

You advised
You cared
You remembered

You were a shoulder
You were an ear
You were always a mouthful

You enjoyed life
You were just you

You hated screeching violins
You loved Freddie Mercury
You did not see grey

You loved the smell of the sea
You pored over photographs

You revolted against perfume
You were the work survivor

You wanted to know
You always showed interest

You could be a pitbull terrier
You could be a guardian angel

You called just to chat
Your laugh roared like no other

Auntie Kettie and Maradona all in one
Your boetie will miss you

We will all miss you
Your loving spirit lives on inside us.

I somehow manage to splutter my poem out and some people knowingly smile at the bits that remind them of Venische's 'tell it like it is' language.

MamLu and Andile: the epitome of closeness.

With family and friends, including Andile's sisters Teaspoon, Nolholho and Groovy in Motherwell, Port Elizabeth.

26. Part of the family

I feel privileged to be part of this wider circle of love and acceptance.

Andile continues to amaze me. In December 2003, within about six weeks of knowing he is living with HIV, he is ready to share with his nearest and dearest family at home in Motherwell, Port Elizabeth. Or is she really well? We sometimes talk about 'Motherunwell' because of its reputation for crime, although the Gaba Street circle area always somehow feels safer because of a strong sense of neighbours looking out for each other.

Andile says:

"I really feel I need to tell my Mom and sisters. Otherwise it's like I'm holding something back from them. Hiding and not being true. And that's not my style."

I ask Andile if he feels strong enough to disclose to them on his own. It doesn't seem like a 'problem' to him. And so he takes it in his stride, with me on the other end of the phone if he needs to chat.

The Mbengashe family seems to have a much more open culture of talking – miles away from my cloistered upbringing, marked by walls and privacy. Is it about a natural sense of *ubuntu* or living in much closer physical proximity and shared space?

MamLu is all heart and soul in response to Andile:

"No, my child. We don't have to worry so much about these things. There's nothing wrong with being as you are. I also get sick. Illness is normal and I know you'll be strong."

Now I know where Andile gets his strength from – besides his own inner reserves.

And so I enter into an arena of knowing, warmth and support when I arrive a week or so later for my first New Year with my new extended family:

There are no more secrets, as they know about my HIV status already. With my consent, Andile has shared first with MamLu, and later with other close family, as I felt he also needed to have their love and support in appreciating what we are dealing with.

We have such fun together, sharing a string of December family birthdays and presents. And I learn that having space isn't necessarily about having loads of physical space. Rather it's about being made to feel at home and being welcomed wholeheartedly into family space. It reminds me of an old wall plaque we used to have up in our Hermanus family holiday house:

"When there is heartroom, there is houseroom."

Andile and I are like naughty kids. Maybe not as naughty as the five young ones in the house. But in our own way we launch into each other in our separate-entrance back room. In silence though, as the still-to-be-completed ceilings are joined to the rest of the house. So we enjoy our need to reconnect physically to the fullest in glorious, muffled, giggling silence!

Our family circle feels so strong. I am made to feel part of the family – there's no sense of being a pale-faced outsider here. How lucky Andile is to feel that he could take his disclosure plunge so soon with little fear of rejection or misunderstanding. I feel privileged to be part of this wider circle of love and acceptance.

•••

My sense of greater wholeness propels me into my next ripple of local family disclosures. My Mom's brother Raymond and his wife Wendy are very understanding and accepting. Cousin Kathy is teary but so warmly supportive. Cousin Avril is caring and compassionate, and well, just her earthy self:

To make things easier for them, I say that they are welcome to tell other family members, as I'd like everyone to know openly, rather than through a whispering 'broken telephone'.

I'm a bit exhausted by all of this, so don't make a point of telling cousin Grant directly. And so he pulls me outside one night at a family gathering:

"Listen, I just want to tell you that *I know*. I bumped into Kathy and she told me about it. I was surprised because I never thought of you as being a promiscuous type of guy going clubbing."

I should have freaked. But knowing my wacky cousin, I am more amused:

"It's okay to say 'HIV', Grant. And there's no need to feel awkward. I'd love to have had the chance to tell you myself."

We chat too about how HIV affects everyone, not just gay men or people who may be a bit promiscuous. Grant is attentive and seems to appreciate my opening up to him:

"Thanks, I don't really know much about these things."

I realise once more:

There is so much awareness-raising work to do in our families and across all communities in our rainbow land.

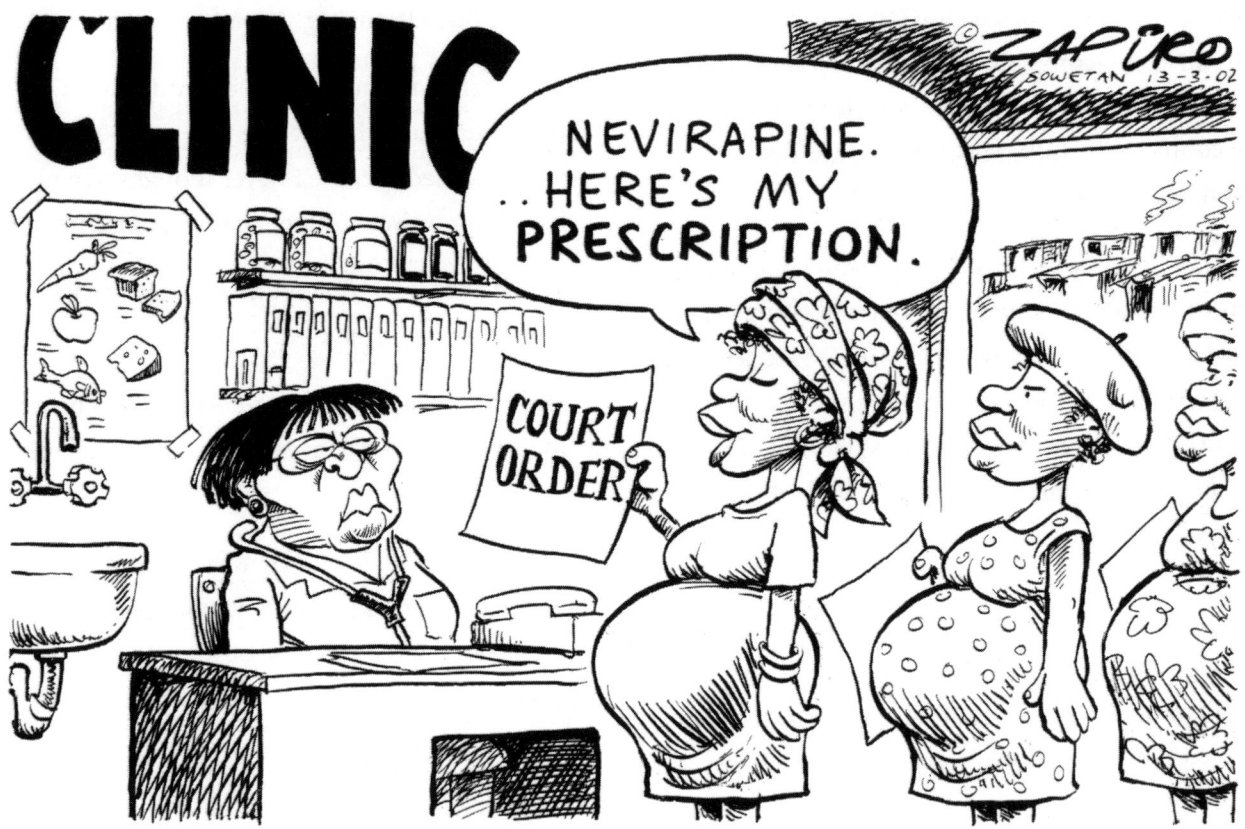

High Court endorses earlier ruling that the Government must provide pregnant women with Nevirapine (Zapiro, Sowetan, 13 March 2002).

27. Let's launch a thousand ships!

We share a stubborn passion for standing up for the human rights of everyone.

Step aside Helen of Troy! My dear friend, Elaine, is the serene face that can launch a thousand ships in South African reality, not Greek mythology. We connected big time during the early toolkit workshops in mid-2002, and our friendship has deepened and blossomed ever since.

Our very different Zambian and South African backgrounds were easily eclipsed by what we had in common. We soon realised that, besides sharing living with HIV, we also share a stubborn, driving passion for standing up for the human rights of everyone, especially of vulnerable groups. I'd spent many years of advocacy fighting for equality for lesbians and gay men, while Elaine had worked closely with and for pregnant moms in causes such as the Mothers-to-Mothers-to-be Project.

I remember Elaine sharing how she was often deflated by a South African Government that seemed to be a stranger to the compassion and urgency required to prevent continued mother-to-child transmission of HIV. A Government that had to be carried kicking and moaning to court by the Treatment Action Campaign (TAC), forcing it to fulfil its constitutional duty to provide access to Nevirapine for pregnant moms and the many thousands of other South Africans needing access to life-saving ARV medication.

Yet Elaine and so many other selfless people like her pressed on regardless and often unnoticed – counselling, caring, awareness-raising and having an impact on the spirit and the lives of individual human beings.

Elaine and I have nursed each other through good times and bad. Through lonely, alone times battling the challenges in our lives. We have shared the trauma of finding a way out of past difficult relationships.

Elaine and I: supporting each other and having fun.

I have such a fresh picture of us sitting together at a garage in Retreat. We are chatting endlessly and giving each other support, while munching on some chips and sipping fruit juice for thought. At that time, Elaine is dreading having to return home nearby to a partner who is simply sponging off her and who refuses to move out, even though their relationship has long since effectively ended:

As people trying to live positively with HIV, we do not need stresses like these in our lives. These pressures, as much as the games HIV plays within our bodies, can cause our energy levels to drop and our mental health to dip.

We share a love of soulful and driving African music. Elaine's face lights up and moves into a transient planet of escape when hearing fresh, new sounds like Senegal's Pape and Cheikh singing *Jello*. And we are in fits of laughter at her spiteful then-partner's confiscation of a music cassette I'd made of her beloved Salif Keita. He is so insecure and threatened that he thinks that Elaine and I are having an affair. I suppose bosom buddies could have a fling, except for the fact that I am gay and Elaine is straight.

Although I hadn't met Andile yet and am potentially available, I beg Elaine to tell her partner that we work together and share a lot around HIV:

"Oh, he knows that!"

"Well then, tell him I'm gay – after all, its not like I'm in the closet, you know!"

"No, I want him to stew a bit. I will not give him the satisfaction of knowing that. It's just pathetic that he can't seem to accept that I have a right to spend time with friends of my choice!"

Thank heavens, in time, Elaine is able to shake off this cloud dogging her life and her efforts to focus on herself, her health and her son, Butler. But it is at the price of having to give up her accommodation and move into humbler digs that require a longer commute into Cape Town for work.

No sign of "clear blue" yet, as Elaine loves to say. But an opportunity to start a joint venture that we have been planning for some time.

Openly Positive's midwives and trustees: yours truly, Elaine, Anne and Andile.

28. The birth of Openly Positive

"We are living with HIV: it's one part of who we are – it doesn't define everything about us."

Sunday lunch in Kommetjie. It's March 2004. The excitement of an idea still to be fully born. We've had loose one-on-ones about starting an independent collective of people living with HIV.

About half my consultancy work involves plain language writing, editing and training. The other half is HIV/AIDS work such as writing, facilitating and developing training materials and workplace policy:

> *I am beginning to feel a strong need to do more of my HIV/AIDS work collectively. It's the kind of work where mutual support is vital and where I feel, in a depressing South African landscape of denial and lack of political leadership on HIV/AIDS, that there is so much more potential to make a stronger impact collectively.*

Elaine is by this stage fuming and very frustrated at not having been paid for many months by the National Association of People Living with HIV and AIDS (NAPWA). A number of NAPWA's best employees are leaving the organisation in search of job security once other opportunities arise.

The NAPWA Head Office appears to be openly siding with the Government's maverick positions, sowing confusion about the effectiveness of ARVs and taking up a public stance of trying to discredit groundswell community mobilisation by the TAC. Gone are the days of powerful NAPWA 'disclosure and acceptance' campaigns. Elaine is burning to put her creative energies into meaningful, independent work.

Our friend, Anne, and my life partner, Andile, help us give birth to Openly Positive. Anne had been doing valuable community development and committed HIV/AIDS work in various community projects and in prisons. She is keen to spread her wings into other sectors, including engaging with workplace programmes in the corporate world.

Andile is busy studying further to advance his range of skills through a personal assistant certificate. While not having had direct organisational experience in HIV/AIDS work, he is passionate about issues such as fighting stigma and discrimination directed at people living with HIV and AIDS.

What does the future hold for us as a new collective? Following a deliberately bottom-up approach, we spend several months and intermittent meetings developing a vision, a mission and a number of exciting early plans. We decide our vision is to:

"Help work towards an easier stigma-free

environment for people living with HIV and AIDS to disclose and to tell our stories, and get access to the care, support and treatment we need."

Ways of achieving this vision include empowering people living with HIV and AIDS to live positively and to develop positive language guidelines to help fight stigma and discrimination. We wish to help shape workplace HIV/AIDS policies and programmes that lead to supportive working environments for people living with and affected by HIV and AIDS.

We sharpen our focus in an organisational planning workshop with the assistance of our friend and ally, Bastienne. By this time, Anne has taken up employment in the National Department of Health with the possibility of improving networking with individuals and organisations of people living with HIV and AIDS, and getting a better understanding of working in government. As Openly Positive is very much a path of exciting opportunities, rather than a source of income and security, perhaps it is inevitable that our initial core group could be drained before we really get going.

Andile is very honest with us. On reflection, he does not feel ready to commit to an organisation that is going to focus on HIV/AIDS education and advocacy. As he is in the process of integrating acceptance of his own HIV status into his life, he feels:

"I think it would be too much for me. I want to be free to focus on other issues too. I don't want it to take over my life. But I'll be there to help you out from time to time."

We understand:

We, too, have to ensure that our personal and working lives are not taken over. After all, our approach is that HIV is but one part of our varied lives.

The withdrawals are a wake-up call. We know Andile's administrative and financial management skills will be valuable at some stage when we need that kind of support. He leaves us a beautiful legacy of a black dove with an olive peace branch flying against a bright orange background. Our fledgling collective has an interim logo. Now Elaine and I have to realistically trim down our ambitions:

"Let's identify a small pilot project to explore working together part-time: let's be very focused and take it one step at a time."

It feels a bit like one of those Agatha Christie thrillers with a lot of fascinating suspects who all drop by the wayside one by one! We have gone from four to three to two. But we have never lost hope in our capacity to make a difference. And to draw in colleagues to assist when there is a need for more capacity.

...

A small manageable opportunity arises for us to cut our teeth as Openly Positive. The Schools Development Unit (SDU) at UCT is developing a video and training material package for use in a number of African countries, including South Africa. The focus is on the empowerment and capacity-building of young people living with and affected by HIV and AIDS.

We are interviewed on video and our stories are used in the training materials. We talk about Openly Positive. We speak about creating supportive spaces for young people in schools and communities. We focus a lot on the importance of self-image and self-acceptance:

> "We are living with, not dying with, HIV. We don't label ourselves 'HIV positive people' – we are living with HIV: it's one part of who we are – it doesn't define everything about us."

Our message is:

> "Be yourself. If you don't know your HIV status, please think about getting tested. You owe it to yourself and those who you love and who love you."

It goes better than I expect. Elaine is a natural on camera, having had much more experience. From her I learn that I need to smile more, not just deliver the 'positive speak'.

The second part of the SDU work is to develop materials for and run an awareness-raising workshop for school educators to help them look inwardly at their own HIV/AIDS attitudes and to become more effective fighters against stigma and discrimination in schools.

The workshop gives us a valuable opportunity to begin developing a central tool of our future work – positive language guidelines from our perspective as people living and experiencing HIV. At the end of the training, we feel we have made a steady start in empowering educators to turn negatives into positives – in their own lives, in their classrooms, in their language and in their interactions with parents in often conservative communities.

While gravely ill, young HIV activist Xolani Nkosi Johnson tries to stir the President into taking the lead on HIV/AIDS – Nkosi died in June 2001 (Zapiro, Sowetan, 10 January 2001).

29. Balancing on the edge

How will history judge our Government of the people?

The emerging national toolkit *To the other side of the mountain – the faces and voices of people living with HIV and AIDS in South Africa* was bubbling and hiccupping along.

Early in 2004, after extensive participatory consultation, the text and design were completed and submitted to the National Department of Health (NDoH) for approval. They didn't have any problems with the content. But one large hurdle loomed on the horizon – they still needed to submit it for approval and sign-off by the Ministry of Health (MoH).

I was churning inside and had been for a long while:

> *Had our democracy in 10 years since 1994 matured to the point where our President, Thabo Mbeki, and in particular our embattled Minister of Health, Manto Tshabalala-Msimang, were ready to celebrate difference? To celebrate the fact that civil society, unlike in many other countries, had the space and freedom to mobilise and publicly pressurise government to implement the promise of our very progressive Constitution?*

About 85% to 90% of our toolkit was uncontroversial and valuable capacity-building and empowerment material aimed especially at us as people living with HIV and AIDS. Naturally, as it was an advocacy toolkit, it made sense to draw on real-life examples of community and other forms of public advocacy to claim essential rights such as access to health care.

This is why, as toolkit editor, I raised with project partner, the POLICY Project, quite early in the process, my concerns about how the MoH would receive examples and quotes that may be perceived as critical of the Government. POLICY Project's position was balanced and reserved, based on previous experience of working with and seeking government approval on a variety of publications. They said:

> "As long as sensitive examples such as TAC mobilisation are used together with a range of other examples and tools of advocacy, there should not be a problem."

I so wish this could be true. After all, people living with HIV had voluntarily shared their hearts and experiences in toolkit development workshops. These included stories about the lack of access to treatment for opportunistic infections and lack of access to ARVs for so many of those of us who needed it over the time period of 2000–2003. This period is significant because it overlapped with the core development of the toolkit from mid-2002 to mid-2003 – exactly the period when so many people were struggling to access desperately needed treatment.

And so we take care in our editing to capture the truth of personal experiences and examples that were part of public and published record for the period that we were doing our best to reflect. But as the storm clouds gather over Pretoria and Cape Town, months slip by with not a word from the MoH or NDoH.

Public pressure is mounting on the Government to introduce a comprehensive approach to the care, support and treatment of people living with HIV and AIDS, including access to ARVs. An estimated 300 people are dying daily. Not people 'out there'. People we know and love.

Does the Government care enough to take the initiative? Not a peep is heard. Deep into 2003, the deaths of our people continue. And so does the criminal neglect of those with the power to begin turning the numbers around. I wonder:

How will history judge our Government of the people? In a word, harshly, when it comes to timeously responding to and managing our HIV/AIDS epidemic.

On a personal level, I feel so torn. I have such proud memories of representing my African National Congress (ANC) branch at the ANC's first conference back on South African soil after its unbanning in 1990. I felt honoured to be part of history and a liberation movement driven by human rights values.

Yet now I feel ashamed and perplexed:

How has our ANC Government under President Mbeki lost the plot so badly on HIV/AIDS? After more than 2 million AIDS-related deaths in South Africa, is saving the lives of our people not the key priority and a national emergency? Will a future change of top leadership give us the direction and political will we need on HIV/AIDS? And take us back to the ANC's roots as a principled liberation movement and a broad church encouraging different views?

(Zapiro, Sowetan, 20 February 2003).

When will the ARV rollout begin? (Zapiro, Sowetan, 21 November 2003).

30. Part of the fabric?

Does this Minister have the right to tell us how to write our history as people living with HIV?

The toolkit day of reckoning? At last a feedback meeting with the MoH in June 2004, almost six months after submitting the text and design. We have a sense of what is coming from comments already made to the POLICY Project.

In the meeting are the project partners: the NDoH, the UNDP, the POLICY Project and their funders, USAID. I am there officially with my toolkit editor hat as part of the POLICY Project team.

More importantly to me, I feel I have a duty to represent the interests of my fellow participants living with HIV and AIDS. Strange, with all the agreed commitment to the UN's GIPA Principle, that no one was invited to formally represent the views of participants living with HIV, who had played a pivotal role in shaping and advising on the toolkit's text and illustrations.

It's a tense environment:

> *Will anyone else in the room have the courage to speak out to support things I may need to say to preserve our toolkit content as it was mandated and developed by our group of project participants living with HIV?*

I quickly learn that no critical or alternative voices will be heard in our meeting room, apart from yours truly.

Representing the Minister of Health is an adviser, who I know from about 15 years earlier when she was a committed activist involved in lobbying for non-discrimination on the basis of sexual orientation in our new South African Constitution. Now she is the close ally and constant voice of our Minister of Health, who is perceived as symbolising the Government dragging its feet on fulfilling its duty to provide urgently needed ARVs to our people.

How ironic that the very Ministry and individuals responsible for the Government's tragic neglect in providing access to treatment are now sitting in judgement over the content of an empowerment toolkit for people living with HIV – the very people who had borne the brunt of the Government's neglect and inertia.

What 'line' will the MoH take? The fun is only beginning as the Minister's adviser launches into a 40-minute monologue to kick off the meeting:

> "I must congratulate you. I come from a teaching background. These are some of the best teaching materials I have seen. They will certainly be easy for community teachers, trainers and service providers to use."

The sugar before the storm? This sounds nice, but actually she is completely missing the main purpose of the toolkit. Its primary target audience is us as people living with HIV and AIDS. For once, we had collectively developed materials to empower ourselves, and to educate and mobilise the next generation of people living with HIV. It is a toolkit by and for people living with HIV – not one written by expert teachers to tell us what we should do, how we should disclose or how we should advocate for our rights.

The Minister's adviser announces:

> "Our main concern is that the toolkit doesn't say enough about what the Government is doing. There is too much emphasis on high-profile court cases involving the TAC opposing the Government. We have no problem with the TAC being mentioned as 'part of the fabric' of the toolkit, but we want this downscaled. We think people will learn more from community examples rather than high-profile examples."

Is the toolkit now meant to be the Government's mouthpiece? People from support groups and organisations such as NAPWA, the Young Positive Living Ambassadors (YPLA) and the TAC had been invited to participate in the toolkit precisely because they represented a spectrum of people living with HIV.

After many years of resisting pressure, the Government had finally agreed to announce a gradual rollout of ARVs in November 2003 as part of its *Comprehensive Plan for the Care, Support and Treatment of HIV and AIDS in South Africa*. The rollout was starting at a trickle in mid-2004, as we sat there. And we were now being asked to publish details of the Government's dramatic response in a publication covering events until mid-2003?

I am trying so hard to keep my editing hat on my now-throbbing heart. I recall how, in the draft of the toolkit's introduction booklet, we have taken great care to be inclusive in sketching the history of people living with HIV in South Africa. Peter Busse, a highly-respected person living with HIV and AIDS for 20 years, had written the first draft of the history, and we have added to it in a caring and inclusive way.

I try to explain:

> "As you know, the toolkit's text was developed in a very participatory and collective way. We were specifically mandated by our closing workshop to write a history that went out of its way to acknowledge all organisations and sectors that

have played a role in shaping the emergence of a growing number of people able to disclose and live openly with HIV.

The reason for including the TAC by name in this history is that the TAC has through its grassroots advocacy played a valuable role in creating space for people to disclose at community level. And this, we hope you agree, is the very purpose of the toolkit – visibility and hearing our voices as people living with HIV and AIDS."

I don't think the Minister's adviser heard me, or perhaps didn't want to hear 'us':

"But you have to understand that mentioning the TAC is very sensitive to the Government. After all, some of their leaders have personally attacked the Minister and the President."

I am churning:

Is it Table Mountain that I can hear rumbling in the background? This is starting to hurt so badly. I get precisely nil support from anyone else in the room – living with HIV or not.

The gravy train is thickening by the minute. The MoH wants a case study of the TAC removed from Tool 5, which deals with advocacy skills. The TAC case study was but one of four case studies – the others dealt with: an example of NAPWA's advocacy work on disclosure and acceptance, advocacy around confidentiality and patient rights, and advocacy in the workplace.

The TAC case study was intended to empower people to learn from the successes and failures of the TAC's public mobilisation around access to treatment:

Was one out of four case studies not 'part of the fabric'? Or was it more about removing critical voices and content that were a bit too close to home for a very vulnerable and threatened Government?

There was still one more big slap in the face waiting for us. Based on the way events unfolded in South Africa in the 1990s, our history of people living with HIV briefly mentioned the role that openly gay men played in opening up space for others to disclose and talk openly about HIV/AIDS. We named Simon Nkoli, Zackie Achmat and Edwin Cameron as pioneers in this respect.

The Minister's adviser comments:

"The Minister would like these names removed. She is not comfortable with us emphasising the links between HIV/AIDS and homosexuality."

I feel sick:

Has the Minister's adviser temporarily forgotten her activist roots in fighting for the equality clause in our new Constitution?

Simon would probably be turning in his grave. Watching our skirmishes from above and wondering: "Is this the Government and struggle that I went on trial at Delmas with Terror Lekota, Popo Molefe and others to fight for?"

I have a nightmarish vision:

Is this the return of the Publications Board-type censorship of the bad old apartheid days? Is this not censorship-by-stealth behind closed doors? Does this Minister have the right to tell us how to write our history as people living with HIV? Who to mention and who to leave out?

Watching my musical granny, Cesária Évora, in concert.

31. Time out for some sanity

Is this the Government I helped to struggle for over so many years? I need a break from this madness for a while.

Some very tough ethical dilemmas are looming for me:

> *Do I place my sub-contracted editing duties above my principles as a human being and my responsibilities as a person living with HIV to other people living with HIV?*

I will face these challenges in August 2004 on my return from Andile and I embarking on our first long-awaited travels together abroad. I know I will return more refreshed to tackle what feels like a circus-juggling act – how to balance directives from the Minister with truthfully capturing our history and on-the-ground activism as experienced by myself and so many colleagues.

I now realise:

> *I will need to begin confiding in colleagues living with HIV and other role-players in the toolkit process on a confidential basis. I can no longer carry this burden alone. Do I hear a bell ringing from my past?*

But first to the pleasure of escaping for a while from our uniquely South African-induced form of madness and denial. As Andile and I fly away, I wonder just how people like the Minister of Health and her adviser manage to sleep at night. Maybe they don't.

There's nothing quite as satisfying as travelling and experiencing a fresh space with the person you love. Paris in summer is more like Paris in winter – it rains almost every day. So not much 'va va voom' weatherwise – the slogan from the funny car advert with our favourite soccer player, Thierry Henry.

Still, the romantic city opens its arms to us. It even clears up enough for us to attend a rock music festival at the local racecourse. An out-of-place but awesome attraction is my musical granny, Cesária Évora, in front of her adoring French fans. Being fanatics, we booked on the Internet from the South African side.

We go to the designated stage about half an hour before her gig and are amazed to find about 10 rows of starry-eyed fans already waiting. I almost feel aggrieved – how can anyone on the planet be an even more devoted fan than I? This feeling quickly fades as soon as she opens her set – effortlessness and perfection take over. I am crying and we hold hands tightly throughout *Bésame mucho (Kiss me lots)*.

London is busy as usual and such a pleasure to share – so much to do and so little time to do it in. Andile connects warmly with friends and family, and this makes me feel very good. We even make time for an out-of-season trip to Highbury, home of my beloved Arsenal. There is a special photo exhibition on to celebrate Arsenal's double winning season of 2003/4.

We spend a warm day with long-standing South African friend, Fran, down in Greenwich. Many hours chatting and catching up in a typically English pub, and enjoying a boat trip on the Thames.

Sharing the WOMAD music festival in Reading is a fitting end to our trip. We treat ourselves to soothing swims and relaxing moments in the *jacuzzi* of our hotel, aptly called 'Renaissance'.

I feel like a rejuvenated soul and do not really cherish the thought of returning to troubled waters.

The bigger picture – the exclusion of critical voices, such as the TAC and the AIDS Law Project (Zapiro, Independent Newspapers, 11 April 2006).

32. Shingles strikes

It's time to take stock of my life.

Soon after returning home, I am contractually bound to complete the unhappy task of making changes to the fabric of our toolkit. I try so hard to keep the integrity of the original document, even though some of its faces and voices are effectively being watered down through circumstances beyond my control. This is my horror movie!

I make certain changes – on principle, I refuse to make others. I try to stick to some non-negotiables, like not changing the original words of our group when speaking from their personal and organisational experiences:

> *I feel that, if we have to compromise to meet the demands of a Ministry pulling the strings from behind the scenes, then this should be limited to commentary and additional examples used, if at all possible. And that they should not be allowed to edit our personal stories and quotes.*

It's not so nice feeling like a puppet being manipulated by unseen hands. True to form, the Ministry of Health will be the handler hiding behind its department. In the end, we will be the puppets on public display – the participants, writers, facilitators and advisers that will be associated with a distorted version of our recent history as people living with HIV.

Maybe it's not surprising what is waiting for me around the corner in what often seems to be my unlucky month – August. It starts on a weekend late in the month – itchiness around my belly button and on my right side. Then come little pimples that within a day flare into blisters in a rather unattractive belt going around my right side to the middle of my back.

I start to feel pain and get to Johnny, my general doctor, after two days. What I don't know is that I've lost very valuable time. It is shingles – my first direct experience of *herpes zoster*, a viral infection that can spread like wildfire if you don't catch it early enough. Johnny consults with Steve and I am immediately zapped onto Acyclovir, a strong antiviral medication to contain the shingles and prevent it from spreading further.

Two months from hell follow. Enormous, immobilising pain (post-herpetic neuralgia) limits my mobility and capacity to be active and work. I am put on Amitriptyline. Huge dollops of soothing cream ease things a bit, but I will have to grit my teeth and get through this somehow.

Andile's love and support is at my side. As is the encouragement and love of family and friends, but I don't really want to see anyone. I feel so uncomfortable. I struggle to sleep. I can only get some rest on my back or my left side and even this takes so much effort.

So, where did my shingles come from? That's a question I still don't know the definite answer to. But what I do believe is that it was partly linked to stress from the burden I'd been carrying with my ethical dilemmas around the toolkit.

Deep down is the uneasy sense that a big part of it could be attributed to my immune system weakening. It is very likely that my HIV decided to take advantage of an opportunity to strike when I was vulnerable. I'd been off ARVs for two years, so maybe my inner message was:

> *Hi, just to let you know we're alive and kicking in here. Maybe it's time for you to take stock of your life. Just a friendly wake-up call from your constant HIV companion!*

Our wedding invite (design by Carol Burmeister).

33. Planning our big day

I have a beautiful shining light to plan for on the horizon ahead.

The Amitriptyline doses at night are making me feel very groggy in the mornings. I have to take this powerful medication every night for about six weeks to help restore the tissue damage caused by the shingles. Foggy mornings become the norm both inside me and outside at misty Kommetjie.

At least I have a beautiful shining light to plan for on the horizon ahead. Andile and I have begun the intricate but fun task of planning for our Commitment Day on 12 December 2004.

South African law hadn't yet quite caught up with our progressive Constitution. Gay couples couldn't get legally married in the official eye of the law.

But we feel we are ready to make a lifelong commitment:

It is the personal commitment between us that matters most, not so much its formal recognition by marriage law.

So our wedding plans go full steam ahead. We briefly toy with the idea of a Cape Town ceremony (for the bulk of my clan and friends) and an Eastern Cape celebration (for most of Andile's nearest and dearest). But very soon we decide that the whole point and symbolism of our commitment is to bring together our respective families and friends. Some of them already know each other, while others have not yet had the chance to meet.

We want a simple, meaningful ceremony at home by the sea and aim to keep our total number of guests under 100 to make our special day intimate. And also because our space is limited. We are going to spoil ourselves and take some of the load off our shoulders by getting an event organiser to manage and oversee the big things.

Our close friend, Giles, a veritable source of information on events and lots more, recommends Lorraine, an ex-colleague now working for herself. We go the 'three quotes' route, getting two more visits and quotes from other companies, all brimming with ideas and eager to organise our big day.

While Lorraine has the personal touch, I am not convinced. She leaves us a thoughtful box of samples and goodies, including a tiny Ndebele fertility doll – a hint for two gay boys to make history by magically producing offspring, I wonder! A nice touch – pity that the accompanying note, box and initial quote is labelled *Patrick and Andile*. Patrick?

What happened to me, Derrick? This is a real turn-off, but as usual, Andile persuades me:

I still don't know how he does it, but I pride myself on being defiantly stubborn on such things. Well, the rest as they say is history, but I'd love to share it with you all the same.

Lorraine is an inspired choice and it is as a team that we head forth to plan all the Ms – the menu, marquee, music, minister and madame facilitators. We give it our personal touch by doing the invitation list and invites ourselves – people are invited to dress "cool, colourful and casual".

With joy and precision, we plan to bring about 30 family and friends to Cape Town from Port Elizabeth, East London and Joburg. We do our very best to balance the numbers – family and friends, Andile's connections and mine, mutual friends who can double up as entertainers, work colleagues and so on. It's hard to leave people out, but we have to make some tough choices.

We love choosing our *Vuyisana nathi – Celebrate with us* CD of favourite songs to be made into a gift for everyone to share the day with us. We help set up a programme for the day, leaving space for plenty of surprises. Thankfully we reach a point a few weeks before when we are able to let go and leave much of the final run-in to our dedicated and loving organisers, facilitators, entertainers, families and friends:

What do they have in store for us?

Any method in their madness? (Zapiro, Mail & Guardian, 15 May 2003)

34. The sledgehammer censors

"We will continue to tell our stories proudly and in our words...
We are not a political football."

Sorry to spoil the fun, but I promise we'll get to that in happy detail. First, there is the little matter of the final toolkit showdown to deal with in my working life. Three and a half months pass before we get the next reaction from the Ministry of Health to the latest changes made – by their standards, quite a quick turnaround time.

As editor, I am summoned to a meeting with the POLICY Project in mid-November 2004, together with our production manager and designer. Nothing is sent to us in writing beforehand, as had been the practice – not a good sign:

Is the latest news so bad that it can only be conveyed face-to-face in a meeting?

In a word, yes! No more talk about 'part of the fabric'. No more suggestions for cuts and trims here and there. This time an order, surprisingly *in writing*, instructing a series of cuts that amount to the full-on political censoring of our toolkit, especially its introduction booklet (with its history of people living with HIV) and the tool on advocacy. And to a lesser extent, the tools on disclosure and human rights. The tools on communication skills (authored by me) and facilitation skills, being of a more capacity-building nature, are largely untouched.

I say *surprisingly* in writing because up to this point the MoH has avoided putting their concerns in writing. But, significantly, we are only given a hard copy of the changes, not an electronic version that would be easier to copy and distribute. How convenient! There is some method in their madness.

And madness it is. Here is a little sample. The MoH order us to remove all mention of the TAC – they are to be removed from the main text commentary, from quotes, from illustrations, from photos, even from resource lists and contact numbers. I take out my imaginary wand:

Now, open your eyes, children – we are going to use some magic to pretend that the leading HIV/AIDS advocacy organisation in South Africa simply doesn't exist.

No, this is not a magician's performance at a children's party, but a real-life tragedy being played out, courtesy of the Government. No more pretence about *high-profile* versus *community* figures, as mentioned in the June meeting.

Documenting the TAC's community and public mobilisation is just too sensitive for the MoH. Yet they had invited toolkit participants in on good faith, including people with TAC connections, and gave birth to a toolkit that is now too hot to handle.

So, like their National Party predecessors with their infamous Publications Control Board, it is into the laager! Remove all pictures of Zackie Achmat, the TAC leader who has caused Government severe embarrassment by highlighting their indefensible positions on access to treatment. Cut references to a leading judge, Edwin Cameron, who has been very critical of Government's denialism and lack of urgency in rolling out ARVs. Sadly, they wish to remove Edwin, still today the only person holding high public office in South Africa to have the courage to disclose that he has been living with HIV and AIDS.

All this in a toolkit designed to encourage visibility and openness around living with HIV. And with a judge ultimately appointed by and answerable in a formal sense to the Government. Their pettiness has reached new levels – we have to remove or change the names of court cases mentioning the TAC. Yet these are used in other public documents and are part of public court records.

No, this does not matter. Even material, for example on Edwin Cameron, sourced from the NDoH's own previous publications, has to be removed. Consistency is apparently not a relevant issue. Once again, I am forced to immerse myself in the sordid task of trying to make sense of these orders from above. This is becoming increasingly untenable – and battle lines are unfortunately being drawn.

So as to fulfil my contractual obligations, I do a technical job of making changes that I feel able to make, although even this is highly uncomfortable. I still hang on to my receding boundaries, such as refusing to make cuts to direct quotes from toolkit participants.

How do I deal with this on a personal level?

The last thing I need while recovering from shingles is more stress. But it doesn't seem as if the project partners care very much about stress caused to people living with HIV through this initially uplifting but now damaging and insensitive process.

I respond to my higher calling and responsibility to fellow people living with HIV and toolkit participants. I have been pushed too far. As the only person in the inner toolkit circle who seems to be safeguarding the interests of participants living with HIV, I feel a duty to consult and to decide collectively on a response.

I recall how, in our opening toolkit workshop, Kevin, one of our facilitators, helped us understand that the process of developing the toolkit, and having a sense of ownership by people living with

HIV, was just as important as its end product. What started out as a consultative process has become a mockery. It is 18 months since the vast majority of participants have seen the toolkit's text.

It is time to lift the veil on dishonesty and deceit. We decide collectively to have a last big go at exhausting internal channels to persuade the project partners to consult with all toolkit participants on the changes that have been directed to be made to our toolkit.

We form a concerned group of 30 toolkit participants and on 29 November 2004 send a detailed memo outlining our process and content concerns to the MoH and the project partners. We call for a consultative meeting to resolve the issues of difference. We mark our memo *not for distribution* in the hope that the powers-that-be will be prepared to meet us halfway as a way of rescuing the integrity of the toolkit and of avoiding damaging publicity.

We end our memo with an impassioned call for us to return to the spirit behind the toolkit:

> "We will continue to tell our stories proudly and in our words. And in a way that consciously includes all people living with HIV and AIDS. Our stories are our faces and our voices. We will not allow them to be manipulated. We are not a political football.
>
> We have expressed ourselves by speaking, by writing, by sharing, by crying, by advising, by facilitating, by living positively, by editing and by sharing all over again in the extended family of friends that the toolkit nurtured.
>
> As our toolkit humbly ends off, 'there is much work to be done' to ensure that we see 'clear blue' again.
>
> By going back to the true spirit of the toolkit and the GIPA Principle, we can still walk this road to the other side of the mountain together. As a concerned group, we all wish that the toolkit again becomes a resource that we 'own' and are proud of – a toolkit that is in name and in reality *by and for all people living with HIV and AIDS*."

No acknowledgement of our memo is received. But there is an urgency in the air – a little birdie has told us that the Minister intends to sign off the toolkit on 15 December 2004.

At our Hermanus family memorial bench: Mama Selina, Andrea, Dad, cousin Avril, her daughters Michelle and Lara, and Uncle Max.

35. Outfits, rings and vows

"I love you and always will with all my heart."

My resentment at having to deal with the toolkit burden runs deep:

All I want to do is to focus on our Commitment Day that is a precious two weeks away. And that's what I resolve to do!

It is time to finalise really important things like what we are going to wear. One of Elaine's many talents is clothes-making. A little way back, she had offered to make our outfits, so the three of us go off on a fun expedition to choose colours of the traditional *umbhaco* fabric. We zoom in on the bright lime green immediately – the question is: who gets the green? I see myself as more of a 'greeny' person, but in a gesture of considerable gallantry I say Andile can be the green man if that's what he wants.

I go for an unusual bright orange: well, for me anyway. No one will be able to say we are not "cool, colourful and casual"! Elaine measures us in all the vital spots and works on an idea for the design. Amazingly, without knowing what we'd chosen for our rings, she comes up with themes that perfectly mirror our ring choices – Andile with a squarish pocket trim and mine a more angled, triangle look. Elaine adds a stunning final touch to surprise us – cowrie shells, the symbol of our house that we featured on our invites.

We have so much fun designing our commitment rings with Leoni, a local jeweller. It feels special to shape and create our own rings, rather than buying them ready-made. Andile chooses yellow gold with two square diamonds and I go for white gold with two diamond-shaped stones. As with our outfits, variations on the same theme, but with a twist of difference – *vive la différence!*

For our ceremony, we decide to go non-denominational. But we keep in elements of rituals that we like, such as binding our scrolls and the repeating of vows. We ask Paul to be our commitment ceremony facilitator – a special connection for me, as he is a long-time friend and also the first friend I disclosed my HIV status to back in 2001.

Preparation is a challenge for Paul too. He is more used to doing services and commitments according to rituals of the Christian faith in his role as a reverend in the gay Hope and Unity Metropolitan Community Church in Joburg. In keeping with the spirit of the day, we create our own personal vows that we will alternate and repeat in English and isiXhosa, preceded by different messages to each other.

We try to capture the essence of our commitment in a few words:

"I love you
and always will
with all my heart.

*Ndiyakuthanda
kwaye ndiyakuhlala ndikuthanda
ngentliziyo yam yonke.*

As my life partner,
I promise to be there for you,
to look after you,
to live positively with you
and to laugh with you.

*Njengo bambo lwam,
ndiyathembisa ukuba
ndiyakusoloko ndinawe,
ndikunakekele,
ndiphile impilo entle nawe
kwaye ndihleke nawe.*"

For the facilitation of the day, we choose a wonderful pair – Groovy, Andile's sister, who I feel very close to, and our friend, Bastienne, who Andile had warmed to in a big way. What a team! They get on like a house on fire when they meet and quickly get down to planning and plotting about a month before the big day. We somehow know their different styles will blend beautifully – Groovy, a confident, outgoing union organiser based in East London, and Basti, a wise and very experienced facilitator of training and assorted events.

This is also the time of a meeting that has been a long time coming. It's Sunday morning at my Dad's place in Claremont – and a precious meeting between MamLu and Groovy, and my Dad and Josephine. A funny coincidence, because MamLu is a veteran domestic worker in nearby Bishopscourt, the suburb where I'd grown up with my parents under the watchful eye of Mama Selina, my nanny, who'd been with my family for over 40 years before her retirement a few years earlier.

We also invite Mama Selina to join us for our big day and she is thrilled to be part of it. Believe me, she and MamLu had more than a few stories to share about 'little Andile' and 'naughty Derrick'. And the way they've grown up!

Our shell, sand, seaweed and stone commitment circle.

36. The day before

We can feel the anticipation in the air.

The final run-up to our Commitment Day starts early in the week of 6 December 2004. There are so many little things to check on – flowers, final transport arrangements for people who are not mobile, and loading up the house with plenty of food and electricity for peak traffic in the days ahead. We are getting a little nervy but feel excited. And wondering how everything will come together under Lorraine's beady eye.

The immediate build-up begins on the Friday when MamLu joins us to stay for the weekend. The first group of Eastern Capers is due on Saturday morning, and they are staying with us – Andile's sisters Groovy, Nolholho and Teaspoon, together with nieces Sinako and Jet. We've organised kombis and drivers to transport people back and forth for the weekend to relieve pressure on us, and to ease worries about drinking and driving.

Everyone is so excited to arrive, especially the young ones when they try on their beautiful *umbhaco* outfits, also designed by Elaine. Our guestroom quickly becomes a fashion ramp and dressing room.

The house is in various stages of reorganisation, with a hectic schedule of deliveries and setting up by Pantsula (our sound and marquee people) and Food Fanatics (our food specialists). With lots of juggling, we manage to fit in nine large round tables that will soon be decked out with Lorraine's handmade colourful African-style cloth and napkins.

Next to arrive are part of the Joburg contingent – Paul, Daisy and Zanele. Daisy is our mutual friend, who has been part of our toolkit group with Elaine and me. We are thrilled that she can make it, together with her partner Zanele, as this has been in the balance. Daisy has been ill with TB and weakish of late. With much encouragement, she has for a long time been on the verge of going onto ARVs to boost her immune system. So she isn't anywhere near full strength, but the fact that she is determined to come down to Cape Town we hope is a good sign.

Andile and I steal a few moments to have a mini-rehearsal with Paul – our only opportunity before the big moment. We work out how we will integrate our rings into the ceremony with colour-coded boxes to be handled by my Dad and MamLu. We each have one remaining parent and they are going to effectively be our 'best man' and 'best woman', and do the honours of handing over our rings.

We do a quick sound check on our voices – Andile is asked to speak up a little as his voice is a bit soft.

Without the emotion of the day, I am doing okay on the projection front – at this stage…

Next is such a treasured moment in our collective preparation. Nic, Becca and my nephews Dylan and Jacob arrive. Together with Sinako and Jet, the kids start building our commitment circle – something we'd taken much joy in planning with Lorraine. Off they go to the beach to collect a load of sand. And together they lovingly create the circle within the beautiful white stones Lorraine has brought. Nic adds his usual creative touch of seaweed. And we will with much pride add a carefully chosen, highly colourful selection of my late Mom's shell collection: this will be our finishing touch on the Sunday morning.

Then a poignant, peaceful interlude sitting on our balcony and chatting a little with Paul, Daisy and Zanele. A moment frozen in time taking in our surroundings and being together. A lull before everyone else arrives. Daisy needs to rest. I remember now how beautiful she and Zanele looked dozing on our bed – within minutes they are far away in dreamland.

There are the wonderful helping hands of family preparing food for the final big contingent of people arriving by bus on the Saturday evening. I don't think the nearby Beaufort B&B in Fish Hoek has been quite the same since – surely change for the better! The elderly residents there are in for an exciting culture shock as the vibrant, excited group of family and friends descend, bringing many a breath of fresh air from Port Elizabeth and East London.

We can feel the anticipation in the air:

Will the weather gods be kind to us on Sunday? Our only real worry is the wind, as rain isn't very likely at this time of year. Although you never quite know in Cape Town, or Kommetjie for that matter, where you often experience the joys of four seasons in one day.

Walking up the beach path with Sinako, Jacob, Jet and Dylan en route to our commitment circle.

37. Celebrating our love

A sense of warmth and love is all around us.

Sunday 12 December dawns a beautiful day! A hint of a light breeze may even refresh us and revive us when we need a pick-me-up. It's impossible to sleep in with our heads buzzing and a zillion bits of preparation happening all around us.

Adding Mom's shells to our circle is sublime. Andile's sister, Teaspoon, artfully paints our faces – an option all our guests will have on arrival. Then on to the balcony for some photos before our planned escape to a secret waiting spot. A couple of birds perch on a new tree outside as I write this – that's where we were then, floating a little as we felt our butterflies before the flight that awaited us.

Our guests were invited for *12h30 for 13h00*. We picture people arriving as we sit sipping our fruit smoothies at Kommetjie's local surfers' café. It seems weird not to be there, so we have to settle as imaginary flies on the wall:

> *Becca, Bastienne and their group are playing gentle jazz as background music, while our guests mingle and enjoy nibbles off braai fires. Some are Kommetjie regulars, others visiting us for the first time – another reason why we want our day to be very much 'at home'.*

Lorraine collects us at 13h15 to take us to our secret rendezvous. Teaspoon is on call to touch up our face-painting that has had to put up with our sweat and forgetfulness. Or should I say mine, in classic *Mr Bean* fashion, as I tried to wipe my perspiring face. We make our way down the beach path to our meeting point behind the dunes, still concealed from the house and those waiting for our grand entrance.

This is a touch we have planned so carefully. A vision we had one dusky evening:

> *Wouldn't it be beautiful if we are led up the winding fynbos beach path to our house by children from our family?*

So we meet on the beach to be wired for sound. And waiting excitedly for us are Sinako, Jet, Dylan and Jacob – the boys wearing Elaine's *umbhaco* sashes to blend in with the girls' outfits. As we link hands with Andile and me at the back of the procession, I am already choking with emotion. I can just hear the strains of the band playing Abdullah Ibrahim's *The Wedding* to welcome us.

Dylan leads the way. The wandering walk is so beautiful. I grip Andile's hand, wondering how I will get through this without collapsing in a dizzy cloud of elation. As we near the gate, I start recognising happy, welcoming faces. This is really happening!

Ululating, piano chords, excited shouts, clapping, violin strains and the jingle of Venetia's bell as the gate opens. And into the commitment circle we step. The children sit on the ground around the circle. MamLu and my Dad sit expectantly in colourful garb, waiting alongside us within touching distance. Paul moves in behind us ready to start, beautifully robed.

A sense of warmth and love is all around us. Like the feeling you get when you sit facing the sun and close your eyes – a sea of crimson and orange:

> *Is that a waterfall I hear or just the sea adding atmosphere? I feel I'm going to cry very soon, while Andile seems so composed, concentrating and cleverly avoiding eye contact with our world looking on.*

Paul welcomes everyone and explains the commitment ceremony they are about to witness. He switches between English and isiZulu throughout the ceremony to make everyone feel part of our moment:

> *My whole life is flashing in front of me. I'm feeling very focused and very emotional.*

Paul calls on Andile and me to exchange our messages and vows. Andile will share his vows first in isiXhosa and then in English. And I'll go in English, followed by isiXhosa. Andile is so clear and firm. Gone are his nerves from our rehearsal yesterday. We are holding hands gently:

> "Thank you for loving me. Thank you for making me believe in love again."

I feel it so deep down when Andile vows:

> "I promise to be there for you, to look after you."

Now it's my turn. Or so I think. The first instalment of a wonderful, unexpected theme for the day – water! Of the teary variety. I just can't control myself – and I don't want to. I try a couple of times to start my message, but my tears take over. Comic relief from Paul: "tears of joy", he says with a naughty smile.

Andile is now holding my hands tightly as if to encourage me to get the first words out. Finally I do, launching with some relief into my few words. With another little pause and choke when I say to Andile:

> "Thank you for giving me back my life."

I feel so strongly at this moment that I am the one so privileged to love again – unconditionally and joyfully. I use the words from the very first love card Andile gave me:

"Our relationship may be different from what others think it should be. But that really doesn't matter because we know it's right for us. With you I can always be me and that makes me love you even more."

It feels so right to say, "I promise to live positively with you":

This is our way of including living openly with HIV as one part of our lives and as one of our commitments. We truly believe, and do to this day, that a huge part of being positive and living positively is supporting each other and sharing healthy, loving souls.

We then exchange the scrolls with our vows. Binding the scrolls is a pair of very old, family silver table-napkin rings engraved with our names. These date back to before I made my way into the world – it somehow feels we are carrying a piece of history and a part of my dear Mom into our joint future.

Paul calls on MamLu to bless our union with a message as a family elder and as Andile's Mom. MamLu speaks about the joy of seeing Andile happy and settled:

"Mabhuti, you have found a home here in Kommetjie. I have seen how you love each other. You must please look after Derrick and also take care of Derrick's family."

We feel like a big, extended family already. As our family elder and as my father, Dad echoes MamLu's blessings:

"I wish to bless you and Andile. Have dignity in life. Have dignity in love. Look after each other. I wish you both great health and happiness on this wonderful day."

Paul symbolically strengthens our union by binding the scrolls together. My eye notices a small but significant little hitch about to happen. MamLu and my Dad have been given the wrong ring boxes. I give a delicate signal in sign language, hoping no one will notice. This feels preciously relevant, as Andile has much bigger fingers than me. I have visions of his ring slipping off my dainty finger into the soft sand and seaweed of our commitment circle.

All is well. Better than well. We cherish exchanging rings, wanting the moment to last forever. Paul declares us married through our commitment to each other. And invites us to have our first kiss. Soft and virginal it was too – if you believe that, well then you'll believe anything!

We are radiating happiness. We are feeling honoured. We are feeling so touched in the presence of so many loved ones. As we leave the commitment circle to celebrate, our choice of song throbs in the sea-air – McCoy Mrubata's beautiful instrumental *Mr and Mrs Adonis*, a dedication to his grandparents. The inspiring sounds carry us into a wave of hugs, petals, kisses, hellos, pats and shrieks. We greet, we thank, we laugh, we sway, we cry, we are ourselves and the party has started.

Paul binds our message scrolls and blesses us.

High Court and later Constitutional Court judgements pave the way to legalised same-sex marriages (Zapiro, Sowetan, 8 December 2004).

38. Water, water everywhere

"Happiness... starts here and now."

Salif Keita, Malian singer

Basti and Groovy are ruling the roost as our co-facilitators. We are floating along. Rotating from table to table. Enjoying starter nibbles. Becca and Basti's group Strings Attached are soothing our ears once more.

Groovy shares how Andile became her brother as part of an extended family. Sister Zet has some words of wisdom for the blushing young couple:

"I want to address you on the road of marriage. Marriage is a two-way street. It's about respect and communication."

Drifting away now to the operatic strains of our friend Mjiko singing *Panis Angelicus*. And we're all laughing along to the carefree singing, chanting and dancing of the young ones: Sinako, Jet and Nopinkie. More Eastern Cape harmonies from dear family and friends and then a repeated call:

"Andile, Andile!"

Water is pouring from our downstairs loo basin all over the tiled floor. *Amanzi kwakhona!* Chaotic rushing about, mopping up and evacuation of two inside tables.

Out of the blessing of water, courtesy of a burst tap, comes some wild, energetic dancing in a circle, mirroring our commitment circle of shells and seaweed. An unannounced special touch – Andile and I are draped in a large duvet – a gift as part of a full bedroom set to keep us warm. We are traditionally blessed afresh with much song and dance. Finally our patient, tipsy loved ones feast on a delayed main course:

It's almost like we're back on land after being out at sea on our water festival.

Nic continues with the ship theme: this is crazy – it can't all have been planned:

"We wish you a wonderful relationship, and much companionship and friendship – and don't forget to leave your battleship in the harbour."

Andrea blesses us too, and in her participatory style gets everyone to join in a dedication to us:

"We, as family and friends of Andile and Derrick, gather together today to affirm your commitment to each other, and to wish you both everything you need to make your future together a fulfilling, loving and caring partnership."

An old friend, Maphelo, dedicates Brenda Fassie's *Nobody loves you like I do* to us. Teaspoon says our togetherness has shown her the true meaning of love. We are feeling so lucky and happy.

Elaine puts in a beaming performance, modestly shrugging off her designer label. She has everyone in giggles when she starts off:

> "I'm so happy for the two of you. Standing here as the three of us, it almost feels like I'm also getting married today."

We feel her words. Just like we feel the presence and warmth of everyone.

Time to cut our tiered cake, adorned with marzipan shells and somehow set off against the Hout Bay mountains peeping out from beneath our Bedouin tent. Andile nonchalantly tastes bits of cake – to rescue them from falling of course. We cut the gorgeous mound together, while the kids are nobly offering to taste!

It's our turn to respond and we get a chance to share some slightly light-headed thank yous. We decide to do it together in turns and without notes. We forget a few people on our mental lists, but no one seems to mind.

This is a poignant moment to celebrate all those with us and especially dear, departed people who are with us in such strong spirit – Andile's Granny Nowinile, his brother Mkhangeli, my Mom Moyra, friend Venetia and my Aunt Lucy, who as a cook supreme would have been so proud of the food.

There's a lovely interlude to wander on the beach in the pinky-blue evening dusk. To take some photos and have a short breather. And then to jive to the pulsating voices, chords and beats of Maphelo's African jazz band, especially assembled for our day. Many coffees, drinks, chats, chocolates and *ciaos* later, we are left to reflect on a perfect, dreamy day.

When I think of 12 December 2004 now, my mind races. We swell with pride. Yes, Malian singing legend, Salif Keita, was spot on when he said:

> "Happiness isn't for tomorrow... It starts here and now."

Jointly cutting our shelly wedding cake.

How we felt the next morning.

39. The after party

I'm enjoying the moment.

When we stumble to bed that night, another little surprise awaits us. Our bed is made with the duvet and trimmings we'd paraded with earlier in our day. A loving, unseen family touch. Andile is in dreamland by the time I join him in wedded bliss. Oh well, he's collapsed on top of the duvet. So let's try that out: it's summer after all!

Our party of visiting family and friends joins us on Monday from the B&B to give our festivities a real long weekend feel. Lots of scrumptious leftovers that we can now properly taste and enjoy. A picnic lunch for all on the lawn in the sun. Meanders on the beach and a few bold loved ones venture into the icy Atlantic waves.

Back at home, little Pepe decides my hair needs a brush – with a twist that only a small innocent thing can get away with. I'm lost in conversation before I realise she's combing my locks with the hand brush being used to tidy up our water festival-decorated stoep floor:

> *They're all laughing at me and I'm enjoying the moment.*

Animated chats, gaping yawns and smilingly reminiscing all those 'did you see' and 'you must have heard' moments from the day before. The first of a series of loved ones are being transported to airports and bus stations. Then more goodbyes. Daisy is promising she'll be going onto ARVs very soon. We wave and shout:

> "Of course we'll be sending you the photos. Let us know you arrived safely."

A sigh of exhaustion for us! Thank goodness we have left the Tuesday open for more tidying up and recovery space, for we will be up at an ungodly hour on Wednesday to begin our long-awaited *businyanga* – our word for *honeymoon*.

Manto 'doctored Aids kit'

Group told to drop gays, activists and high-profile figures

By Kerry Cullinan
Health-e News Service

The Ministry of Health has doctored an HIV/Aids guide to remove references to the Treatment Action Campaign and gays, and to cut out photos of Patricia de Lille and men who disclosed that they were living with HIV.

The only reason for this, the letter suggests, was that the ministry "wished to avoid links being made between HIV and homosexuality".

The Star, 15 December 2004.

40. Thulamela

We feel a sense of belonging.

Minister 'doctored AIDS kit' blazes out at us from *The Star* newspaper at Joburg airport. A little reminder that we are still on Planet Earth – what a pity:

Has someone broken ranks, got fed up and leaked our internal toolkit memo to the press? Or has an investigative journalist sniffed out the story that has been brewing for so long?

I'd tried so hard to keep it under wraps in the naïve belief we'd get a humane response. It's sad to see it out in the open in this way. Sadder still is the response from the Minister's adviser. Half denial, half lies. Some waffle about how they didn't see how a focus on "high profile people" could help those in the community waiting to devour our toolkit.

The response doesn't seem to matter so much and is a mild irritant – like the mosquitoes waiting for us in the game reserve. Our focus is solely on winding down and wallowing in gorgeous nature as we make our way to the Kruger Park's Satara camp. It's the first visit to the park for both of us. We take in some welcoming four-legged souls on the way to our thatched hut on the perimeter of one of the thankfully quieter Kruger spots.

We feel a sense of belonging, to each other and in deference to the beauty of an African night twinkling with birds and stars. We make a big fire and have a special toast. A small candle pays homage to the anniversary of losing Venetia – it's 16 December. And, as they say, *iindlovu* like us seldom forget.

It's very restful to have so little planned. There's a vague sense that we'll take a drive sometime in the morning before it gets too hot. We are greeted by friendly buck, zebra and even a rare rhino camouflaged in the bush. We take turns to drive. Andile decides it's safer to park some way beyond our first bull elephant grazing at the roadside! I learn the delightful and very apt isiXhosa word for giraffe – *indlulamthi*, the one that goes over the trees. They seem to have so much time – I think I'd like to live like that.

We soak up three sleepy days filled with healthy *siestas* and exploring the wilds in our own time. We are glad we decided to do one organised night drive. Spine-tingling and unique night sounds. And an exciting ending – a pride of lions retreating into the bush caught fleetingly in the spotlight.

And then we drift on to the jewel of our *businyanga* – spoiling ourselves for a couple of delectable nights at *Thulamela*, meaning a *place of rest* about an hour's drive from the Kruger Park.

We've booked a log cabin hidden in the trees with a misty view over the green landscape and our own spa bath on the balcony.

It's totally private and blissfully peaceful. A space to be alone and thoroughly lazy. To make our own food. To jog and breathe in country fresh air. To be acknowledged by our hosts with a complimentary bottle of wine when they hear it's our honeymoon.

Hmm… we must have another final, slow dip into the spa to say farewell to the tweeting birds in the rustling treetops. And then the Gidana-Fines will head back to our haven at the southern tip – or the *Giddy-Fines*, as we call ourselves for fun when feeling happy.

Daisy (front left) in happy times on our Commitment Day, with Noxolo, Nomfundo, Elaine, Zanele and Butler.

41. In a daze

For once the ocean can't soothe me…

Gorgeous, creative, moving moments. We're back at home developing our wedding message book. Artfully arranging pictures from our special day in a big black album. It's fun deciding on the spreads, combinations, sizes, colour splashes and little mementos. Our DVD is divine and we can't wait to share pictures and memories with loved ones who were with us. And with those who couldn't be there to capture the feeling and the spirit.

We continue to hear funny Commitment Day anecdotes. At a children's party, friends ask my eight-year old nephew, Jacob, what he did on the weekend of our big day. Jacob replies:

"Oh, I went to a gay wedding!"

But the early months of 2005 are not all wine and roses. Daisy has taken a downward turn. She made such an effort to be with us in December. It sounds like it was the last time she was feeling well and happy. Zanele sounds so down. With support from Elaine, Nomampondo, Jason, Nomfundo, many other friends and myself, Zanele is trying to be strong.

It's so hard. We all tried in different ways to encourage Daisy to get onto ARVs as soon as possible. Now she's so weak. She's tired all the time and coughing a lot. Yes, she's on TB treatment. Surely it's possible to save her – there are TB medications that are compatible with ARVs.

She's certainly not getting the back-up she needs from her employers, NAPWA – a caretaker of the rights and well-being of people living with HIV and AIDS? As with Elaine's battles before she found fresh, reliable employment at the beginning of 2005, Daisy hasn't been paid for many months. I wonder:

How is she supposed to buy food, pay rent and get the medicines she needs?

Daisy needs support from everyone to take the tough road onto ARVs, even at this late stage. As part of the unfolding South African tragedy, we hear that Daisy has been discouraged from going onto "toxic" ARVs. Sounds like our denialist President Thabo Mbeki speaking, or our Minister of Health of beetroot and African potato fame. Beetroot red she should be for influencing and shaping the views of those discouraging Daisy from taking ARVs.

It seems as if Daisy is fading fast. I speak to her on the phone one day. She sounds hoarse and exhausted. Has she lost her will to fight on? Zanele is getting more and more down. And desperate.

At last, a beacon of light? Daisy will be moved to another hospital where ARVs are available "next week". But next week never comes. Daisy leaves us on 5 March 2005, telling Zanele that she really loves her.

Andile is there for me. We are there for each other. We try to be there for Zanele – how do you begin to console someone who has lost a partner? We are there for Elaine – how do you ever replace a friend like Daisy? We are angry too – we didn't have to lose her.

I sit in endless silence on the balcony, just feeling dull and sad. For once the ocean can't soothe me, as I try to express the emptiness I am feeling:

In a daze

The sun sets on a dark day
Why Daisy why?
How can Zanele ever fill your space
Your grace
Your pride?

Yes, you came back into the light
Bravely out of the shadows
But we needed you
For longer
For much longer

Why didn't you give yourself
That chance
To get stronger again
And be your sparkling self
Once more?

We will miss you
So sadly
With some anger
Because you deserve to still be here
In person

Although in spirit
Dear Daisy
You will always be part of us
And your memory will shine
Deep within our souls.

42. Very low and a little high

We are celebrating Peter's life while Daisy looks down on us from the heavens.

It's a sad, deep reflective week:

In Daisy, we've lost a soft and loving friend. We've lost a dedicated fighter for the rights of people living with HIV and AIDS. We've lost a role model standing up for the dignity of women and of lesbians and gay men.

With a queer twist of irony, I remember how Daisy's impish sense of humour used to refer to "PDAs" – *people dying with AIDS*. In our positive language work, Elaine and I always speak of people *living with HIV* and *living with AIDS* because now there's so much hope with access to ARVs. But not for Miss Daisy. I used to love calling her "Driving Miss Daisy". This always made her giggle.

Andile and I go up to Joburg for the funeral on Saturday, 12 March. We stay with Paul and JP. It's Andile, Paul and I travelling together again. Not this time in our commitment circle, but to pay tribute to Daisy. I can still so clearly picture her smiling face and the presence of her soul in Kommetjie. We even got her to dance on 12 December.

The vigil, service and funeral are gruelling. She brings so many people together to reflect and remember who we have lost. It's a sad reunion for a bunch of us bound together by the toolkit and our friendship and admiration for Daisy.

Zanele's strength is awesome. She has the dignity and poignant presence to sing *Amazing Grace* dedicated to Daisy at the church service. Her voice moves me deeply. We know beneath her deep tones is human fragility. She will need so much support afterwards when the crowds have gone.

Daisy, as usual, has the last word. She had decided she wanted a formal funeral. Not an activist one. True to her quiet dignity and commitment, there are no banners. Only a powerful sense of togetherness and plenty of peaceful reminiscing at the 'after tears' at her sister's place in Vosloorus.

Up-and-down times these are. Within two weeks, we are back in Joburg, this time for a joyous celebration. Our friend Peter is celebrating 20 years of living with HIV. From the time he was diagnosed in 1985 – through his years living in Swaziland to his admirable positive living advocacy work in South Africa – he has been a true role model for many.

Now on ARVs and living life to the full, Peter even mentions giving up his heavy smoking. One of my little missions has been to persuade him in this direction – I feel driven by the memory of my Mom's mouth cancer induced by 30 to 40 'ciggies' a day.

Andile and I stay with friends, David and Mags, in Westdene. It's lovely spending time together and travelling as a team to Peter's imaginative party in the old Johannesburg Observatory. There are trapeze acts, heartfelt speeches and choir harmonies. And the inspiring voice of Musa Njoko, South Africa's first gospel singer to openly disclose and dedicate a song to living positively and long with HIV.

It's a strange feeling:

We are celebrating Peter's life and wishing him many years of positive, long life. And knowing that Daisy is looking down on us from the heavens.

We spend a precious evening with Zanele. We watch parts of our Commitment Day DVD together. We focus on Daisy's presence. Her smile, her vibrancy. It's a living record for Zanele. We leave a copy with her. Very small we know, but at least it's a special something to console her loss, her emptiness, just a little.

Uncle Max and Aunt Lucy at their Golden Wedding celebration.

43. Uncle Max releases me

It's time to show our faces and voices.

Elaine and I are ready to make a big leap forward. We'd put in an application to do an Openly Positive skills development workshop at the South African AIDS Conference. It's held every two years and the next one's coming up from 7–10 June 2005 in Durban. We are successful – it's to be a big step for us onto a much larger stage.

We will present a workshop on *Positive language in HIV/AIDS communication*. We are breaking new ground. From our perspective and experience as people living with HIV, we wish to equip others to use positive, empowering language to help overcome stigma. We begin developing specific guidelines, with examples of how to turn negatives into positives when we speak and write.

It's a wonderful advocacy opportunity to influence the language and attitudes of health care professionals and others. As people living with HIV, we will help to shape powerful guidelines that we will evolve further after feedback from people living with HIV and other role-players in the field. We want to move away from being silent, closeted "sufferers" and "victims" to being living voices helping in a small, but significant way to change the face of the HIV/AIDS epidemic.

I use the image of moving out of the shadows into the light to capture our need to become more visible:

Out of the shadows

Keeping up with news
Of infected suffering victims
Unfeeling, unwelcome, deadly names
Framed by pens that think they know
How it feels to be alive

Time to show
Our faces
Our voices
Our names
Telling tales of positive living
Letting them know
How it feels to be alive.

Although my dear Uncle Max may have asked:

"Why all this activism and fire now?"

Let me explain. Uncle Max was the husband of Aunt Lucy, my Dad's sister, who we remembered so vividly on our wedding day. In 1988 at the age of 75, she passed away from heart and kidney failure after she had been living with emphysema.

Uncle Max used to call me "blondie" after my golden boyhood curls. He would grab my cheek affectionately and say: "hey, blondie". Actually, it was a little sore but I knew he meant well.

Uncle Max was a remarkable 91-year old. He'd been our family doctor for many years – one of that rare breed of old general practitioners who did house visits and really cared. Sometimes, perhaps a little bit too much. When one of us had a cold, we would jokingly say:

> "Are you going to have a visit from Uncle Max? He'll probably confine you to bed for a week. And maybe even admit you to hospital."

Uncle Max fell ill on his 91st birthday on 28 November 2004. He was then confined to bed. A number of his vital body functions were simply slowing down. Naturally.

He sent a loving message and apology for not being with us on our 12 December Commitment Day in Kommetjie:

> "It's too far. And it's too hot. But I promise to come and visit you very soon."

Such was his spirit. His version of positive living at 91. He never did manage to visit us. We are rather at his bedside in Sea Point. Sometimes I call with Andile, sometimes with Nic or Andrea. Sometimes alone.

Usually I visit in the presence of cousin Avril, Max's daughter. Together with her daughters, Lara and Michelle, Avie has a special, warm loving bond with her Dad. With help from a full-time carer eventually, they carry the burden and the joy of constantly being at Uncle Max's side. Yet it is hard for him, as such a fit and independent man for so long, to be nursed and cared for.

He'd often reminisce with me what a wonderful life he'd had. How grateful he was for the love and support of his family. And he'd say with a big beam:

> "To be surrounded by all these loving, marvellous women!"

Max's mind stays active until the last. He has always been an extraordinary reservoir of knowledge and wisdom. He took us on drives near Hermanus as kids to see the wreck of the Birkenhead at Danger Point and to patiently explain how waves are formed in the sea when we asked endless questions.

Then, as now, he always followed our activities and thoughts attentively. He showed great interest in my human rights and plain language work, and in my HIV/AIDS activism, although I never had the opportunity to disclose to him, as I had done to Avril, her husband Norman and the younger family.

One day, early in 2005 during a visit, Uncle Max says to me:

> "Now that South Africa is free, you must be living a free life. My boy, you no longer need to serve the nation. You can enjoy life."

A lovely thought! But there are still "causes to be defended", I gently share with my dear uncle.

44. A heavy month of passing

I cry for the second time that morning.

I often wonder what Aunt Lucy would have said and thought. She knew about my sexuality even though I'd never formally come out to her. We'd have little conversations about 'this and that' when she took a pause from her amazing skill at solving crossword puzzles. Or between hands as we played casino or Portuguese rummy together in Hermanus. Aunt Lucy taught me the art of doing my daily fix – the *Cape Times* crossword.

Of course, not the *straight*, quick clues for me! Rather the *cryptic* ones, needing a suitably bent mind to unravel them. I subconsciously think of her every day as I place one of her devices on my crossword – a dividing line to separate new or hyphenated words.

She would have been so proud of Uncle Max's newfound domestic independence. Aunt Lucy once said, as passed on through family oral history by Avril:

"The most he ever does in the kitchen is put the kettle on."

Well, deep into his 80s, Uncle Max moved into a flat after selling the "too big" old family house. And there he proudly learnt to cook and invited us over in turns to savour his recently acquired culinary skills. These skills were a new addition to his devotion to being the extended family's handyman for so many years in his earlier life. Nothing was too much trouble – picture frames, plugs, leaks and any other kind of repairs.

Visits to Uncle Max become shorter. He is getting tired so quickly now. We still have short, meaningful chats. And it feels so peaceful to hold his hand as he drifts off into his much needed rest. Flashes of my Mom as her active, daylight hours diminished. But like Max, when she was 'with us' she illuminated the room and you had her total focus.

Unexpectedly, Mom's shadow is waiting around the corner. The one thing we can expect from this life is the unexpected. Sister Andrea has been experiencing discomfort and some fatigue. She tells Nic and me on the phone. She's had some tests and yes, she has a lump on her right breast that will have to be removed. I close my eyes and hope:

Please, let them catch it early. Ands, you're too young to even think about following in Mom's footsteps.

Ands is 55. She sounds scared. But we will be there for her. Her partner, Nicola, will be at her side all the time. First, she needs support to tell Dad. How will he cope hearing about the vulnerability of another of his children? Like Uncle Max, he's chugging along solidly at 83. He assures Andrea that he and Josephine will be there for her. Andrea's fighting spirit kicks in. She will show much fortitude as she negotiates six weeks of draining radiotherapy from mid-June onwards.

It strikes me how automatically and candidly she was able to tell us that she was living with cancer. No delay for stigma here. Immediate support on call as it should be! I wonder why living with HIV has been so different:

> Would I have been able to disclose sooner and received the support I needed quicker in 2005? Will it be different in future for others like me? And those unlike me who live in communities and environments where stigma is still high?

The creeping shadows of May 2005 are far from over. I get caught up in a working world deadline. On 27 May, I manage to submit my plain language edit of the first draft of a health handbook for the AIDS Law Project at Wits University.

My inner voice tells me I want to find a space to visit Uncle Max again. It's Monday lunchtime 30 May. I'm with Avril at Max's side. I feel like I'm saying goodbye to him. Avie has a sense of peace. Maybe she too has said her final goodbye. He's physically colder now, although the warmth of what he has meant to all of us lives on endlessly.

It's Tuesday morning around 09h00. The phone rings. I can feel Andrea's voice: it's not about what she is bravely facing. It's a resigned tone of sadness. Uncle Max passed away peacefully in the early hours of this morning. I cry tears of relief. His was a good life. Family calls continue and we decide we will meet up at Avril's in the afternoon.

It's moved on to about 11h00 now. My work phone rings. It sounds like a voice from the past. Who is this? It is Nono, my ex Thulani's young niece. I last spoke to her, aged around 13, about seven years before. She was a sweet little soul, who so much enjoyed a maiden trip to Cape Town to stay with us in Gardens:

> "It's me, Nono. I've just found your cell number on Thulani's old sim card. Thulani passed away on Sunday. He was very ill for the past few months."

I go into another kind of daze. Silence explains itself. As we had agreed, I stopped supporting Thulani with money for his ARVs once public access to treatment began. Yet we had kept in occasional touch on the phone every couple of months or so.

We chatted briefly around New Year 2005, the last time I heard his voice. He phoned to tell me he was moving up to Port Alfred, the extended family home where he had always felt most at home.

I remember I tried to call him after losing Daisy in early March. I'd felt the need to call all the people I knew that I'd been close to and who were in various stages of HIV progression. No response from Thulani's cell. Had it been stolen? Had he sold it? They had no landline in Port Alfred.

It feels like the clouds are moving in on me. I cry for the second time that morning:

> *This time it's sadness – frustration maybe at what might have been. At the loss of another life to HIV and AIDS. I wonder if I could have done more. But later I am to discover, devastatingly, that Thulani had made particular choices that no one could have saved him from.*

For now I feel alone. Andile is at college and will be back in a while. Basti is there for me on the phone. It always feels good to off-load on her insatiable capacity to listen, to probe and to empathise. Later on, Andile leaves me one of his beautiful notes with these touching words:

"My dear Derrick, I am terribly sorry for the loss of both Uncle Max and Thulani. I know how hurtful it is to lose someone close to you. I know you cared for them so much but there's nothing you could have done to stop their passing. I think that you must celebrate the fact that you've known them. Think of all the beautiful and lovely things you have done with them. I want you to know that I love you through happy and sad times."

A breath of fresh air: Madiba's moral leadership around HIV/AIDS in talking openly about losing his son (Zapiro, Sowetan, 11 January 2005).

45. Rising from the dead

"Things are not as they seem…"

Elaine and I wow people at the Durban Conference. We have to adapt our positive language workshop really fast. We've been expecting 50 to 60 people – closer to 200 attend. We speak from our hearts about personal experiences of negative, stigmatising language like "HIV sufferers" and "AIDS carriers". We get participants to work in small groups, using examples from press clips, to develop their own ways of changing sensationalist, stereotyping language into positive, empowering language. We pilot our novel 12 guidelines to guide positive language use.

We use examples very close to home:

"Why is the conference called 'the South African *AIDS Conference*', not the '*HIV/AIDS Conference*'? Shouldn't we be inclusive of the vast majority of people living only with HIV? People who, with support, care and treatment, may never progress to living with AIDS."

We spend the nicest, informal sharing moments in the curiously titled 'PLHA lounge' – a quiet space for people living with HIV and AIDS, away from the endless talking heads spouting PowerPoint research wisdoms and medical jargon about "HIV patients" and "research cohorts". Sounds like we are little pieces in a children's game of battleships:

Yes, we begin to realise that our positive language mission to change attitudes is a longer-term crusade rather than an overnight process.

But it is a distracted week. Behind the human reconnections is the sinking feeling of what is awaiting me on Saturday 11 June – Thulani's funeral in Port Alfred. Talk about down to earth from the theory and occasional practice of Durban's conference halls… I feel I need to be there to say goodbye, to have my own closure to a traumatic period of my recent life.

As I drive down from East London, I wonder who I will get any emotional support from. I know the set-up in Port Alfred. No one is working. It is a life of struggle. I'd decided to book into a local hotel so as not to burden the family. And somewhat naïvely as it turned out, I'd already assisted with covering a chunk of the funeral costs. I console myself thinking:

At least Thulani deserves the dignity of a proper, warm funeral.

I make my own way to NEMATO – the Nelson Mandela Township of Port Alfred. People had proudly renamed it after Madiba – what a pleasure: at least he is a leader we can look up to as a role model around HIV/AIDS through the work of his

Children's Foundation and his openness about losing his son, Makgatho, to an AIDS-related illness.

On arrival, I greet and hug Nono and her brother Vusi, and pass on my condolences and wishes of much strength. I know how close they were to Thulani.

I wonder if I'll know anyone else as I go into the inner room where family is traditionally seated on the ground ready to pray, sing and mourn through the night. I'm not that easily shocked, but what is awaiting me chills me once more as I try to write about it.

I'm ready to greet the people gathered and show my compassion and support for their loss. I see an old woman before me. I think:

A remarkable resemblance to Thulani's late Mom – a look-alike sister? Or is this his Mom: can this really be happening?

His Mom, I was told, passed away some years earlier – Thulani said that she had been killed in a drunken brawl. I recall because I helped out with funeral and other costs even though this was after we separated in 2000. When I heard this devastating news on the phone, I believed it. I didn't ask for copies of the undertaker's quote at such a time.

I'm feeling sick. I've been lied to. I've been used. It gets worse. Next to his Mom, who has risen from the dead, is Angelina, Thulani's little niece, who he told me had died in a taxi accident:

Were these just flights of fantasy from a person living with depression or did he deliberately aim to deceive me?

Next there is Thandiswa, a younger sister, who lives with a mental disability. She is also meant to have departed this earth. I've had enough for now and ask to talk to Nono and Vusi in another room. On enquiry, Vusi declares uneasily and with acidic irony:

"Things are not as they seem. But please don't be angry. We don't want you to get upset."

It's clear from our conversation that these deaths have been made up to get sympathy and financial support. Being lied to and deceived is one of the deepest cuts in life, and this isn't over yet. There are still two more phantom deaths from the eight years I'd known Thulani. There's an older sister, Vuyiswa, reputedly dead from stab wounds – she makes an appearance later that evening.

And Mara, a cousin and close friend of Thulani, who often nursed and looked after him. He'd told me that she had passed away too from an AIDS-related death. Well, she rose from the dead the next morning too – actually we had a nice hug and chat. Ever hugged a ghost before? Something stopped me from saying to her:

"How nice to see you Mara. Actually, Thulani told me you were dead!"

Stepping out of our commitment circle as a married couple.

With our unofficial 'best people' MamLu and Dad on our big day.

Walking on Kommetjie beach as newly-weds.

With family and friends on Kommetjie beach on our wedding day.

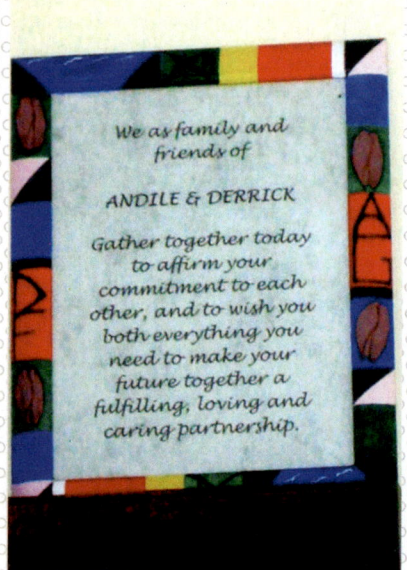

Commitment dedication to us from family and friends, beautifully painted by Nicola, Andrea's partner.

17 November 2005: my birthday supper with Dad and Josephine, Andrea and Nicola, Andile, Nic and Becca – sadly my last with Dad.

A call to awareness and action by our youth, as we remember the carrying of Hector Peterson's body in the 1976 uprisings (Zapiro, Independent Newspapers, 15 June 2006).

46. My message in the mayhem

"Please make sure that you protect yourselves."

I'm still in a semi-trance as I drive to NEMATO again in the morning. I've had a reassuring chat with Andile on the phone on the Friday night, but unsurprisingly I suppose I'm not quite myself. I get lost and have to phone Nono for fresh directions and to meet me.

To almost add insult to injury, I am requested, after the service at the house the night before, to speak in the church funeral service on the Saturday. I remember blankly asking:

"Are you sure you want me to speak?"

I'm abuzz with mixed emotions this funeral morning. I realise that there were deaths Thulani told me about that were true, such as the loss of another sister and a close aunt:

> How to separate fact from fiction? How did I allow myself to be led up the garden path? To trust so easily? I know it doesn't matter now, but are any of these untruths from the time when we were still together? I think the lies about Vuyiswa may have been, but I feel there is no point in going back to diaries to check this out.

I am here now to say goodbye. I am very shaken and so disappointed. Yet I decide to take the opportunity to deliver a message to a church full of mainly young people. To my knowledge, Thulani was open about living with HIV, so here is a chance to turn all the depressing negatives into a positive. I will not speak about *us*. I will talk about *him*. I will talk about what our next generation can do. At least my bizarre presence can serve a purpose.

Before it's my turn to speak, I catch sight of a striking young woman with a little boy child, seated in the same row. I do not know her. She is wearing the same type of bright-green coloured *umbhaco*-style outfit that Andile wore at our wedding. At one point, she breaks down, crying and wailing. She is helped from the church for a little while to recover, but returns to take a seat further back.

I share a little about Thulani, saying that he was a fighter. I try to break the heaviness (my heaviness?) by talking about his love for cats, for stylish clothes and for kids. I launch into my message:

"As young people, you have the opportunity to learn from Thulani's life. Please make sure that you protect yourselves. Don't delay in having an HIV test. It's time to talk openly – no more *amagama amathathu (the three words)* – let's say HIV! No more avoiding what is around us by saying *amagama amane (the four words)* – let's say

AIDS! Let's support each other and all the people living in our community with HIV and AIDS."

I speak in part-isiXhosa, part-English. The rest is translated. I think I strike a chord. I could never have known the need for my words. Like that deep movie *Secrets and Lies*, this real-life screenplay is not yet over…

We're at the graveside now. I had my big cry in the morning when I saw Thulani in his coffin. He looked better than I had imagined with a rather distinguished beard. By now I am feeling more and more emotionally detached.

Two more nails in the coffin. I recognise Abongile at the graveside – Thulani's buddy and an old flame from his younger days. We greet. The can of worms is opening again. It seems that Abongile didn't know Thulani had been living with HIV and AIDS. But he says:

"Did you know Thulani had a child about two years ago with Nandi?"

I am amazed. She was the woman wailing in the church. I am horrified at the thoughts cluttering my head:

Did she know he was HIV positive? Did she take ARVs to prevent mother-to-child transmission?

Has the child been tested? So many questions. No answers.

Back at the house, I watch Nandi and the child. He looks so innocent. Vaguely like Thulani too, although my imagination is by now working overtime. I'm thankful I said my few words in the church – if Nandi didn't know before, I'm hoping she knows now that Thulani had lived with HIV.

As I'm about to make my quick-as-possible getaway after lunch, I'm introduced to the home-based carer, who looked after Thulani in Port Alfred. I can see it more clearly now – he made his choice to return to Port Alfred, the place where he felt most comfortable to live out what he probably knew were the last months of his life.

Having produced a child, was this not something worth living for? The carer tells me that Thulani never revealed that he'd been on ARVs previously in Port Elizabeth. He lost a lot of weight and was increasingly weak in Port Alfred. He was on the waiting list to get ARVs in Port Alfred when he died. I feel so helpless. Perhaps he'd lied to me about his treatment too:

Had he ever been on ARVs in Port Elizabeth? Or did he just take my money to live on and pay off debts?

A final slap in my face. His 'born again' Mom and Thandiswa ask for my phone number. I'm ready to draw the line. I say I came to say goodbye to Thulani. I will not give them my number to bleed me dry any more. I am awake now!

To this day, no one has thanked me for helping out with the funeral. I don't need to be thanked. I have my dignity. I have my life. I am a wiser person.

As I leave NEMATO, I can't wait to return into the arms of my life partner. Our commitment is real. Andile is real. I am closing this chapter of my life.

Relaxing with Fran on Planet Earth.

47. Back on course

It's time to let go of another stressful cloud hanging over me…

Back from Planet Pluto to my everyday world. The Planet Pluto idea is a lovely hangover from days working at South Africa's constitution-making body, the Constitutional Assembly, in 1995. Friend and colleague Fran and I invented *Planet Pluto* to describe crazy and busy periods in our lives. Whenever this happened, we placed a Planet Pluto sign on the door of our shared office.

Andile is nearing the end of his Financial Management diploma course. He will pass with flying colours. We plan an Eastern Cape time-out. Andile will spend precious time with family in Port Elizabeth and I'll join him there later for a few days. Then we venture off to the Grahamstown Festival for three days of wandering, watching, absorbing and relaxing.

We stay at a local B&B – one of many homes that become a refuge for the thousands of festival-lovers at this time of year. We admire the new craze in the streets – mime statuettes of young kids in cabaret-style outfits. They change position and pose whenever a few coins are deposited. We love the Ambie Sistas – an all-women jazz band and talented cast reliving the songs and words of a 1950s diva from Galeshewe, Kimberley, as they make their own way into the showbiz spotlight.

It's a time of rebuilding and securing our solid foundations. Unplanned, this is symbolised by the Mbengashe clan placing a wall and a gate around the family house in Motherwell.

After the stressful Thulani saga, it's time to let go of another stressful cloud hanging over me – the toolkit. Nine months of group pressure and standing up for our rights will finally bear fruit, although there are no real winners in protracted battles of this nature.

By August 2005, the Department of Health has finally agreed to consult and renegotiate consent with our toolkit participant group. Sadly, they decide not to invite other role-players like the facilitators, advisers and writers to the meeting. With the unseen hand of the Ministry of Health still pulling the puppet-strings, they will not budge on content approval issues.

The group itself has reached saturation point. They want the toolkit to get out now, however imperfect it may be. I read the signs and decide, with my editing cap, to make a suggestion to help break the deadlock. I propose the addition of words to the acknowledgements page to reflect the reality that subsequent cuts and changes have been made to the text that were beyond our control as participants living with HIV.

Instead of "Final Editing: National Department of Health", the Department finally agrees to add:

> "Editorial Approval: National Department of Health."

I'm surprised at the 'approval' wording. This conjures up the reality of what has happened rather well:

> *Imagine the Minister and her 'yes madam' adviser sitting with their magnifying glass, scissors and rubber stamp.*

I'm letting go now. No more shingles and unnecessary stress for me. Other individual participants will decide for themselves whether to allow their names to be associated with the final product. My assessment is that about 80% of the toolkit remains true and empowering. People on the ground know the grassroots achievements of the TAC and others in forcing the Government to move on access to treatment. Many other publications and forms of media, some of which I will gladly be part of, will continue to testify to the inspiring work of the Simons, Zackies and Edwins of this world.

After much agonising, I decide to attach my name to the imperfect final product to recognise the two years of slog, inspiration and heartache I have put into the toolkit. Understandably, some contributors decide to withdraw their names, rather than associate with an end product soiled by the Government's political interference and censorship.

Deciding to take back control of my health.

48. Treatment decision time

I've got to put my health first again.

Elaine has been bravely battling some of the side effects of her ARV treatment. She has found the *lipodystrophy* – body fat changes – really hard to manage. Ironically, as I'm moving towards being comfortable with the idea of going back on treatment after three years off, she is beginning a treatment interruption to think through her options.

I worry and think about her, as she feels so close to me. I hope she will find the wisdom in her own time to be strong enough to go back onto a more tolerable ARV combination when she feels ready. I just can't face losing any more close people this year, actually not ever!

With Andile's loving support and the backing of other dear ones, I need to focus on myself now:

I've been through a stressful time of loss. Now I'm determined to find ways of reducing stress and cutting down on my workload. I've got to put my health first again.

My July check-up is crunch time. My CD4 count has dropped steadily by about 80 each time since my shingles setback. My last count was 352. The words of a debate at the Durban Conference about the optimal time to begin treatment are ringing in my ears. While a number of doctors and companies recommend considering going on ARVs with a count between 200 and 350, the official number is below 200 for getting access to ARVs in the public sector.

It's a replay of 1999, but the goalposts have shifted dramatically. No more 'hit hard, hit early'. Rather an approach of delaying treatment until your CD4 count demands it, or because you are experiencing recurring opportunistic infections or an AIDS-defining condition.

In spite of the high stress I've been subjected to, I've been doing relatively well. I feel it's an achievement to have won myself three years off ARVs since August 2002. With the support of my HIV doctor, Steve, I decide I want to take control of my life and my health again. My count is now down to 300, I can afford the medication and their cost has in any event dropped down to around R500 a month. More importantly I feel so strongly:

I don't want to wait until something happens to me, like developing an opportunistic infection.

I tolerated my ARVs relatively well last time around and am ready to take them again. I know the initial period of adjusting to side effects will be tricky, but I am taking a long-term view:

I'm doing this for Andile and all the people I love. I'm doing this for myself – this is my long-term insurance policy.

I now know I'm on ARVs for life. Current medical research is saying that it is not advisable to stop treatment once you start and are tolerating it well.

It's a new combination: 3TC again, but now combined with d4T (Zerit) and Efavirenz (better known as Stocrin). The Stocrin will literally give me nightmares. The first three weeks or so of August 2005 are very tough. Vivid dreams like I've never experienced before, but eventually they wear off. The interesting thing is I'm remembering so much more of my dreams than before.

Foggy mornings and seriously disturbed sleep are hard to live with. I keep saying to myself: "Think of the bigger picture." I do – and it does get better.

Recife, Brazil: no need to move the goalposts.

49. On a bigger stage

In Brazil, civil society and government work together in a committed way.

Life and work carry on, although I have to constantly remind myself:

I have to be strong to stomach blood, liver and kidney tests to check on how my body is attuning to the new treatment. I have to somehow remember to take my medication – now it's two tablets in the morning, two an hour or so before supper, and the one adorable, big Stocrin before lights-out.

I'm relieved to know there are new developments on the horizon all the time. Once it is registered in South Africa, Tenofovir may replace d4T in ARV combinations – thankfully it has less toxicity and long-term side effects. There are hopefully also further options on the way to reduce the pill burden and thus encourage treatment adherence. Two or three tablets once a day may soon become a real possibility.

My first real work test since going back on ARVs is upon me. And it's a big challenge energy-wise. I've been approached by the Joint United Nations Programme on HIV and AIDS (UNAIDS) to be a rapporteur for a UNAIDS-civil society planning meeting in Recife, Brazil. They are especially keen to have a report-writer who is also living with HIV and thus more sensitive to the issues involved.

The work is right up my street. There's a sense of going back to my NGO roots. This is part of a civil society international monitoring initiative to check if governments are carrying out their promises made in the international UNGASS (United Nations General Assembly Special Session on HIV/AIDS) Declaration of 2001. Governments, including South Africa, agreed to work towards a variety of prevention, care and treatment targets. It's an opportunity to play a small part on a much bigger stage, and to hear what role-players, including networks of people living with HIV, are doing in various countries.

The travel is draining – with the various time changes, I'm in transit for around 25 hours either way. Sometimes I feel I don't know what time of day it is. Remembering to take my ARVs and getting the time gaps right is demanding. Just to add to the challenge, Recife is in North-Eastern Brazil and close to the equator, so it's fiercely hot. The sun is up by 05h00 and is at South African midday height and heat by 06h00.

Despite the climate, it's very inspiring connecting with so many committed people. No double agendas here. In countries like Brazil, there is a sharing of objectives between civil society and government. They don't speak with the same voice but they work together in a committed way.

It's a 'mostly work and little play' kind of trip. But I make space for a lively browse around the local market with Kenyan and Canadian colleagues. And for my usual jogs and a long walk on the sand beneath Brazil's legendary palm trees. Soccer goalposts are everywhere – maybe we'll have a real holiday trip to Brazil sometime in the future and take in a live match.

I realise on the way back that I didn't see any Brazil nuts in Recife. Funny this, as Elaine and I always munch them in South Africa – we are told they are good for our HIV.

We're feeling in harmony.

50. A coming together time

"We'll carry your positive living flag."

It's the last quarter of 2005 and I'm feeling on a bit of a Kommetjie wave. I'm doing work that's meaningful. It's integrated with my life and who I am.

I'm excited at connecting with the *Siyayinqoba Beat It!* TV educational series on living positively with HIV. I'm writing website materials, including summaries of the episodes and documentary stories for the Community Health Media Trust, the show's producers. The plain language and positive language sensitivities in my soul are in harmony.

I'm relieved Elaine's back on a new ARV combination and that she's getting along quite well.

I don't often feel I'm floating. I'm feeling whole again, with a strong sense of peace this morning. Andile is in bed doing the 'target' word challenge, as my Mom used to do on the back of her cigarette box. He gets the big word so quickly these days, it's scary. I'm proud of my blossoming co-wordaholic.

Things are coming together for us. Andile's doing part-time 'outside' work and assisting me part-time as my personal assistant. He actually enjoys organising, typing, filing and managing finances. He's reducing my load, and his own, spiritually, physically and emotionally.

As I drift into the day and my crossword falls into place, there's a sense of general achievement, logic and direction. My crossword progress often indicates where my head's at on a given day – some days murky, some days sharp, while most are somewhere in between.

In December 2005, we joyously celebrate the first anniversary of our Commitment Day in Lisbon. It's our first trip to Portugal and we're feeling very settled. A city of hidden treasures, groved walks and beautiful walls of ceramic tiles. We pause during a city tour on our special day at an imposing monument to slaves in Portugal's African colonies. An intimate traditional restaurant honours us that night. The tasty snacks, serene surroundings and gentle *fado* accompaniment tell me our time has come. We are feeling privileged and happy to be one.

Next stop a cosy, but cold time in England. Golders Green is white with snow as we house-sit Ken and Joan's warm space. In Leeds, it's New Year party time with cousins Keith and Tess. It feels good to share experiences with friends of theirs, a couple, who say they were inspired by the DVD of our Commitment Day. They are planning to celebrate their own union in mid-2006 under Britain's new civil partnership law.

Back home, we're settling in to a peaceful 2006 when we receive a very sad and totally unexpected SMS from Jason on 6 January:

"Peter Busse is late."

How is this possible? Our friend Peter was so full of life. He had touched us as a role model. And we'd celebrated his 20 years of living with HIV in 2005 in Johannesburg.

We hear that Peter returned exhausted after extended overseas trips to Thailand and the Netherlands – two of his favourite places for pleasure and work combined, in unique Peter-style. He was hospitalised around Christmas time, and slipped away from us on 6 January with only a few chosen friends and family around him.

I have flashbacks to my many phone calls with Peter. Like Venische, he was one of those special souls you just chatted to without reason and felt comfortable with. He listened. I listened. We were there for each other, never judging, just caring.

Why now Peter, I wonder?

We needed you for longer. Was it treatment fatigue? Could we have persuaded you to stay on your ARVs, instead of stopping for longer than we knew? The attrition of life? You were always there for others, yet perhaps not enough for yourself. You always made your own choices. We will miss you deeply.

Andile and I sadly pen a tribute to Peter for his memorial celebration in Joburg:

To Peter with our love

Peter
You left us so suddenly
Without a wave
No spotlight on you
No centre stage for you

Yet you strode the world
Like a colossus
Fighting stigma
Symbolising positive living
Caring for others

You lit up our world
Empowered us
Always encouraging
Intently listening
As a dignified role model

You gave us strength
Showered us
With your words of wisdom
You were a true survivor
We are proud to have known you

We'll carry your positive living flag
Driven by Buddha Bar sounds
With a farewell wave
A left-handed legacy
To your boundless spirit and good deeds.

As in life, Peter's passing brings so many of us together in memory, in tribute and, in his spirit, to reaffirm our resolve to live positively and to serve others meaningfully for as long as we are able.

All smiles with Peter, Commitment Day, 2004.

Dad and Josephine on their wedding day.

51. Losing Dad

Sitting in the same room that we lost Mom, I feel drained.

We were so very proud to have our Commitment Day blessed by Andile's Mom and my Dad. I feel numb all over again as I strain to reflect on losing my father so suddenly, just two months to the day after we lost Peter.

Thinking back, there was a warning bell. After Dad and Josephine return from their regular trip to London in November 2005, Dad complains for the first time:

> "Deks, I felt cold. It was too cold for me and I didn't feel like the long walks I always love."

Dad is a great walker, be it the Kirstenbosch Botanical Gardens, the Hermanus cliff paths or Regent's Park in London. Josephine is worried, as it is so unlike Dad to complain and not enjoy each moment.

Dad has check-ups and seems to brush this aside as a temporary hiccup. After all, he's an astonishingly fit 84 – mentally and physically. So it's back to the tennis court in January for his weekly game, now down from three sets to a more sane one. We often had to persuade him to take it easy in the heat – typical of Dad to imagine at 80-plus that he's still Martina Navratilova on the circuit at 50.

Then the big reality jolt. It's late January, and Dad has received shattering news after a further check-up. He has pneumonia and is then diagnosed with lung cancer. The tumour is creating water on his lungs. The water can be drained, but is likely to build up again.

Dad's breathing will increasingly be affected and his energy levels will drop. At his age, he will not be strong enough to withstand chemotherapy and this is not recommended.

We are all deeply shaken. Josephine is devastated. We all try to give Dad, Josephine and each other support and comfort. Dad is getting visibly weaker by the day and does not have his usual appetite. We spend precious time together talking and just 'being'. Dad rests more and more.

I think to myself:

He deserves more time. We all want more time with Dad. He must have thought, as we all expected, that he had at least five to 10 more years.

A feverish period of financial and family planning meetings follows. Dad staggers through these altruistically, determined to leave as much in place as possible to ensure our future well-being.

What Dad really needs is more time just to reflect and 'be', and not to have to think and work. But he has always chosen to keep active in this way. His driving energy, generosity and enterprise continue until he has no more energy left.

Like Mom in her last days, Dad just wants to be at home in his own space, away from cold hospital rooms. We sit together on a Friday morning in late-February. Dad is dozing, yet he can feel my hand. In an interlude, we chat briefly and Dad shares some wishes for loved ones he wishes me to help take care of.

I play him some music as he drifts off into a midday *siesta*. He nods in recognition and contentment as Il Divo sing *My way* in Spanish. It's the last song we hear together. As with his beloved Frank Sinatra, Dad truly charted his own wise way.

It's a Monday again, 6 March 2006. Josephine's fateful, heavy call:

"We've lost Dad."

Sitting in the same room and on the same day of the week that we lost Mom in 1991 on the other side of the bed, I feel drained in the knowledge that I'm now officially an orphan. At a later moment of poignancy, I console myself, in positive language style:

I will not label myself a "cancer orphan", even though I'm now parentless after losing both Mom and Dad to the rigours of mouth and lung cancer respectively.

Mom and Dad's tombstones alongside each other: a sense of finality.

52. It's all relative

"You embraced us for what we are and not for what you wished us to be."

Life really is relative. Saying goodbye to Dad and losing him puts a lot of things into perspective. I reflect on the meaning of living and on my life. Work, deadlines and passing daily irritations drift far into the background.

In a brilliant flashback to his 80th birthday celebration, Dad's funeral and wake bring together his family from the varied avenues of his rich life. There are his immediate blood relatives, his warm and loving new family through his marriage to Josephine, his Wynberg school family, his bridge and *klawerjas* family, his tennis family, and his music and concert club family. The list goes on.

Andrea has the strength and grace to speak movingly on behalf of Josephine, Nic and myself. She sums up a lot of what we are feeling as Dad's three children:

> "Many people become more conservative as they grow older. Dad, you continued to grow. All three of us challenged you in different ways and we know that you struggled with many aspects of our lives and the choices we made.
>
> We wish to thank you for the most wonderful gift a father can give his children. You embraced us for what we are and not for what you wished us to be."

Andile and I, together with Andrea, Nicola, Nic and Becca, spend much time with Josephine reminiscing and piecing together the unreality of losing Dad in the space of six weeks. Josephine has opened up to us, and we have opened up to her and her family. Even though Dad was the cement that held us together in life, he will also continue to keep us united in his loving memory.

We struggle to deal with endless estate and related meetings. We don't really want to face all of this. The dissolution of Dad's companies, as well as the distribution of his meticulously preserved shares and investments, feels so irrelevant and mundane in his absence. No more meetings when he held the floor and gently scolded us:

> "Why have you got so much in this account when you could be earning better interest elsewhere?"

As if nurtured and inspired by Dad, Andile and I start a vegetable garden a few days after Dad's funeral. It's part of our positive health ethic and it feels so comforting picking our own peas, radishes and squash. Unofficially, Andile takes on the mantle as 'constant gardener' and yours truly as 'assistant gardener'. While not very green-fingered, this dog is still trying to learn new tricks.

We can't deal with the thought of sorting Dad's things and we leave this for about six months later. As I sit a bit heavy-hearted writing this, I'm wearing a pair of Dad's baggy shorts and that feels comforting.

Much of 2006 passes in a blur and the months seem to merge into one another. They are punctuated with many touching moments in tribute to a life well-lived. Fittingly, a concert at the Baxter Theatre is dedicated to Dad's lifelong commitment to the city's orchestra and concert club. My love of music and culture was nurtured in my Wynberg Boys' Junior School days under the tutelage of principal and teacher Arnold 'Annie' Lorie. Dad's classical music and Mom's theatre work helped to build on this worldly foundation, and I am profoundly grateful for their influences.

...

It's a time for more reflection. I find myself pouring a lot of my emotion and sense of loss into working on a milestone piece *Changing lives for 25 years and counting: HIV professionals living with HIV/AIDS* for the International AIDS Society. It's a background paper for a satellite session at the *AIDS 2006* International AIDS Conference in Toronto. I enjoy developing the paper collectively with a group of HIV/AIDS activist professionals from around the globe – there's a special sense of being a kind of extended international family working towards similar goals.

It's an opportunity to renew connections from my UNAIDS work in Brazil in 2005. More importantly, it allows me to reflect on the collective and individual journeys we have charted over the last 25 years.

The paper aims to commemorate our role as people living with HIV in the global response and to examine progress in implementing the GIPA Principle. It also highlights challenges we have faced as HIV professionals living with HIV and promotes progressive human resource policies to protect our rights.

The paper moves beyond the traditional understanding of the term *professionals* to include all health care providers, community educators and human rights activists, who through voluntary and paid efforts have dedicated much of their professional life to HIV/AIDS work.

Above all, the paper feels like a fitting tribute to Simon, Daisy, Peter and so many others. And a momentary pause and refuelling before renewing our joint efforts, while being inspired by the dear ones we have lost:

"Our ability to be visible as workers and volunteers living with HIV is our most powerful way of challenging stigma and discrimination. We have all known courageous people living with HIV and AIDS who came before us and paved the way for many of us by being open about their status…

In developing a vision for the future, it is important to remember the countless number of HIV professionals living with HIV and AIDS who we have lost. In redoubling our efforts, we believe that our historical, current and future involvement has been and will continue to be essential to the scale-up of prevention and treatment initiatives as part of the global response. Whatever the challenges we face as people living with HIV/AIDS and HIV professionals, we will continue to believe in our ability to save and change lives, and to live long, productive lives."

We enjoy good times with Elaine and Vita in Kommetjie.

Around the fire with Paul and Giles in Hermanus.

The icy Atlantic surprises Vista, Andile and Lhonki during a Kommetjie stroll.

Our gorgeous array of models for Triangle Project's 'Life is for living' booklet, 2006, in Kommetjie (picture by Kelly Walsh).

Poignant memories of Mom while collecting shells in the Seychelles.

Feeling focused and happy: Mauritius, New Year 2007

Urgent need to accelerate the ARV rollout and access to effective, safer medication (Zapiro, Sunday Times, 4 April 2004).

53. No more wasting

"Where's your bum?"

I've been looking at myself in the mirror lately. I've never been one for extended facials and loads of creams. It's a few months into 2006. Numbers-wise I'm doing well. My CD4 count is at 505 and my viral load is 'undetectable' (now measured as below 40). I'm also glad that Andile's CD count is strong at 783.

Andile and I often joke about our bodies and I laugh at him asking me: "Where's your bum?" Up until now, I've put it down to my regular jogs and maturing middle age body changes, and it doesn't bother me. But my increasingly fixated mirror peeps are making me feel more and more self-conscious. My face is visibly wasting – on my cheeks to be precise. And it doesn't help when people awkwardly say:

"You have lost a bit of weight lately."

I do some research to remind myself: it's a side effect of my ARVs, probably the d4T. Not *lipodystrophy* (body fat redistribution), as experienced by many women, but rather *lipoatrophy* (fat wasting) that often is most visible on the face.

It seems unfair. ARVs have been so successful in keeping my HIV dormant and largely inactive. And I don't have any visible signs and symptoms of HIV progression. My cheek wasting is in its early stages, but somehow my cheeks feel like craters and are so visible to my beady eyes:

Yes, I know the benefits of my ARVs far outweigh their limited side effects, but this is still happening to me. I'm driven to do something about it. It's bothering me.

Lately, I've also experienced another, invisible side effect – some mild *peripheral neuropathy*, a known side effect of d4T. I'm feeling a slight tingling in my fingers every now and then. My doctor, Steve, feels this is likely to become more frequent over time if I remain on d4T.

After much consultation, Steve and I agree we should take me off d4T and back onto AZT, using the Combivir combination of 3TC and AZT, together with Stocrin:

"Ideally I'd like to get you onto Tenofovir – it's been available internationally, including in Namibia and Botswana, but is not yet available in South Africa, as it's unregistered here. Tenofovir has a very low side effect profile and is only taken as one tablet once a day."

And so the saga begins of waiting for Tenofovir to be registered by the Medicines Control Council (MCC). Apparently, this is imminent as a 'fast-track' registration that's only supposed to take nine months. Well, the nine months is speedily developing into a delay of three years.

Crazy really when all reputable HIV doctors are recommending Tenofovir as a public sector first regimen ARV:

Will our Ministry and Department of Health ever manage to prioritise the health needs of the bulk of people living with HIV requiring ARV treatment in the public sector?

Shades of my first spell on ARVs with private access – Tenofovir is available privately through a special section 21 application to the MCC to get permission on an individual basis to use Tenofovir for a six-month period. My 'private' ARV package will be around R600 a month, with Tenofovir as part of my three-drug cocktail:

Surely Tenofovir's price can be negotiated down for public sector use once the Government is willing to take the plunge?

I'm getting frustrated. My facial wasting feels like it's getting more and more marked by the day. Is the AZT aggravating it? Steve says taking the AZT will not make a big difference as I wait for my MCC application to be processed:

"It could take anything from a day to a few months. Try not to sweat about it. We'll get it as soon as we can."

But I am sweating and I feel like I don't want to wait. Why do I need to wade through so much bureaucratic red tape to get access to a drug I need now? So I arrange to source an interim supply of Tenofovir from Botswana to get me started and to keep me going for three months.

It feels like such a relief to take my first 3TC, Tenofovir and Stocrin combination. And a big advantage is that I only have to take my medication as four tablets once a day before going to bed at night – so much easier than three times a day and having to remember an early evening dose.

It's just as well I get my interim medication. Steve calls me with a resigned tone about six weeks later:

"I phoned the MCC to check on your section 21 application today. They say they've lost the application. We'll need to re-apply."

And so we do. Planet Pluto strikes once more. Should we be surprised at such a level of incompetence in handling applications for vital medicines?

Another six weeks later, the application is finally approved and, after more red tape, we organise for me to receive my supply via my local pharmacy, together with my other ARVs.

I still have to endure more uncertainty:

Will I receive my supply in time when my emergency one runs out? I am nervous, as the delay could lead to a treatment interruption. As a result, I could possibly develop resistance to my medication.

The pharmacy hears there is a problem with the Tenofovir supply from Bermuda: "The latest shipment never arrived". We wait and get a one-month supply many calls and a few weeks later. This is eventually supplemented by the remaining five-month supply a month or so later in January 2007.

I'm comfortable on my new ARV combination. I haven't experienced any Tenofovir side effects. We are keeping an eye on my kidneys, but so far they are doing well. My CD4 count is up to 602 and my viral load remains below 40 ('undetectable'). Yet there's the gnawing thought of having to re-apply for another six months come the end of April, if Tenofovir is still not licensed in South Africa by then.

I am wishing:

Everyone on ARV treatment in South Africa should have access to Tenofovir as a fallback when they experience side effects or resistance to their ARVs. Or as a first line regimen to reduce side effects sometimes experienced with current first line drugs in the public sector.

Once more, it seems that only public advocacy and pressure by the TAC, the HIV Clinicians Society and other groups will press the Government into quicker than tortoise-like movement forward in accelerating the ARV rollout and access to effective, safer medication.

When bad news is met with love and kindness

My partner's act of courage helped me to confront my fears and take the test, writes **Andile Gidana**

I NEVER thought that I could live with it.

It was in 2003 that I met my current partner, Derrick Fine. I met him through Exit, the gay newspaper. It was love at first sight. I was swept away by his looks, his voice and his warmth.

We started dating from that day and I was always looking forward to seeing him.

The last time I went for an HIV test was in 1996, and I was negative. I never bothered to go again. I just assumed that it would never happen to me. Although I had an inner voice telling me to go and have myself tested, I just ignored it because I was scared.

It was on a Monday that Derrick invited me to his place for the very first time so that we could get to know each other better and spend some quality time together. He sat me down and started telling me about his involvement in HIV/Aids work.

He said the reason why he invited me over was to let me know that he was living with HIV and that he didn't want anything intimate to happen before I knew about his status.

I don't know what happened to me. Instead of freaking out, I was more attached to him. I told him that I loved him and that HIV didn't make any difference.

I could see on his face that he was surprised. I assumed that he thought I was going to reject him. I could feel that he was relieved, and he started crying because he was happy to know that he could still love and be loved in return.

When Derrick disclosed to me, I felt an urge to have myself tested again.

I wanted to know where I stood, and with all the courage and knowledge he gave me, I went for my test in October 2003. The results came back positive.

Funnily enough, I was not devastated — it felt like I was expecting it.

I started thinking to myself that sooner or later I would have to tell my family about my status. It was like a second coming-out, first being gay, and now living with HIV. My mom and I are very close, and I used to visit her at work on weekends. After my HIV diagnosis, it was difficult for me to look her in the eye — I felt like I was living a lie because she didn't know.

I wanted to prepare her, as I knew that she was going home in December. I wanted to use that opportunity to tell her, together with the whole family. To my surprise, she was as strong as ever. She told me that she loves me for who I am and HIV is just like any other disease. She promised to give me all the support I need. My family accepted me, too.

I was relieved and grateful to know that I could count on her and the family as a whole. It is such a breeze for me to disclose now because I know that HIV is manageable and that there is life after HIV.

Derrick and I continue to support each other and we don't let HIV control us — we control it because we are more powerful than it. I just want everyone to know that it is such a relief to get tested sooner rather than later. Believe me, it makes life worth living.

> **It is such a breeze for me to disclose now because I know that HIV is manageable, and that there is life after HIV**

EVERYONE KNOWS SOMEONE

HAPPY ENDING: Derrick Fine and Andile Gidana at their commitment ceremony in December 2004. The couple — and Gidana's family — met news of their HIV-positive status with acceptance and support

Sunday Times, 5 November 2006.

54. Now everyone knows

We don't need to talk about it. Their hugs say more than words.

Living with HIV continues to open up more and more, sometimes unexpected, personal and public spaces to share in and influence others. It feels comfortable for me to participate in a discussion group of people living with HIV and to appear on an SABC1 *Siyayinqoba Beat It!* episode on how the media responds to and shapes our ideas and actions around HIV/AIDS.

And it's a media opportunity that moves Andile to action, with me in a supporting role. The *Sunday Times* has helped to open up dialogue on HIV with its *Everyone knows someone* campaign. Proud and courageous weekly stories from a wide variety of people living with and affected by HIV and AIDS move my dearest to share his story. There is a waiting list of people bursting to tell their stories. The campaign is undoubtedly reducing stigma, although there is still a way to go, as a number of storytellers do not reveal their names or faces.

Andile tells his story openly and visibly when it is eventually published in November 2006 under the title:

> "When bad news is met with love and kindness – my partner's act of courage helped me to confront my fears and take the test, writes Andile Gidana."

The story appears next to a happy shot of us on our Commitment Day. We want to give out a positive image of living with HIV, with committed love between gay men across the 'colour line' for good measure. Andile closes with:

> "It is such a breeze for me to disclose now because I know that HIV is manageable and that there is life after HIV. Derrick and I continue to support each other and we don't let HIV control us – we control it because we are more powerful than it. I just want everyone to know that it is such a relief to get tested sooner rather than later. Believe me, it makes life worth living."

The only downside is that the mini-colour picture introducing the article appears on the page of an obituary to the finger-wagging epitome of apartheid South Africa, PW Botha. Oh well, we can't always choose the company we keep.

For months on end, we get nothing but positive feedback and affirmation from family, friends and work colleagues. While co-facilitating an ancillary health care course at False Bay College, Andile uses the article as an awareness-raising tool to get students talking and, more importantly, HIV testing.

There are positive, unplanned spin-offs. Becca and

Nic use the opportunity of Andile's article to talk to nephews Dylan and Jacob about 'us'. The boys ask questions and are reassured by hearing our news in a warm and affirming environment. I feel so comfortable knowing that they know. We'd both said to Nic and Becca that we'd like them to tell the boys at the right time. I don't know if it's my imagination, but the next time I hug Dylan and Jacob it feels especially warm. We don't need to talk about it. Their hugs say more than words.

I get responses to the *Sunday Times* article from unexpected sources. An old friend, Siyabulela, calls from Joburg to commend us for our courage. Siyabulela and I attended Lizo's funeral together in 2001. I'd wanted to tell him for ages that I am living with HIV but haven't had the right space to do it in. So it's a relief he knows. On the phone Siyabulela says:

> "Thanks guys, you've inspired my partner and me to get tested to check on our HIV status. We've both been putting it off for too long now."

Chris is an old school prefect colleague from over 30 years back. We've seen each other briefly over the years at Wynberg Boys' High School events and reunions. I'm surprised and heartened to get his call:

> "Derrick, just wanted to say that I respect you for having the courage to be open. It's important. And I wish you all strength."

This leads to a nice spin-off chat with the school principal, Keith Richardson, and an offer to do info sessions or workshops with staff and learners on HIV issues. Keith, my Latin teacher way back in 1976, and I continue to interact over a new bursary at Wynberg from the Azriel and Moyra Fine Foundation in honour of our family link to the school. He hasn't taken me up yet on the HIV intervention, but I'm hoping doors remain open:

Strange how seemingly unrelated connections from our past find a way of intertwining and creating opportunities to make a difference.

Joint pamphlet endorsed by Triangle Project, AIDS Law Project, TAC, Habonim, The Equality Project and the Durban Lesbian and Gay Community Centre (design by Doret Ferreira).

55. Will you marry me?

I feel I've come full circle from our advocacy to include sexual orientation in our new Constitution.

Andile and I feel like we are married already in all but name. We made our real commitment to each other in December 2004 in the presence of so many family and friends. And yet we've always thought: it would be nice to have our union officially and legally recognised. No more being told after filling in Portuguese visa application forms:

> "You can't refer to each other as 'spouse' because the Department of Home Affairs has no record of your marriage. You'll have to come in again and correct your application forms, or else we can't process your visas. We are sorry but have to follow the law."

Opportunity knocks in 2006 with a concerted campaign by lesbian/gay organisations to have same-sex marriages recognised in South African law. Our Constitutional Court, in a landmark judgement at the end of 2005, gave Parliament one year until 1 December 2006 to pass legislation giving effect to same-sex marriages on an equal footing to heterosexual unions.

In a frenzied attempt to meet the Constitutional Court deadline, the Department of Home Affairs proposes a Civil Union Bill to introduce the parallel institution of a *civil partnership* for same-sex couples. This looks like a compromise to appease the dogged opposition of many religious fundamentalists and traditional leaders to any recognition of same-sex unions:

> *Have these forces forgotten the spirit and promise of our new Constitution in outlawing unfair discrimination based on sexual orientation and many other grounds? Is there any valid reason why, as same-sex couples, we should not enjoy the status, benefits and responsibilities of heterosexual couples?*

Triangle Project and a network of organisations engage nationally in a flurry of activities, including much lobbying and advocacy, as well as public hearings on the proposed Bill. Andile and I get involved in letter-writing and picketing, and allow one of our Commitment Day photos to be used in a pamphlet calling for support for our constitutional right to same-sex marriage.

We are subjected to much hate speech in the public hearings and debates. I wonder:

> *Why is there so much hate and intolerance from so-called civilised voices in the church and other quarters? Why are they so threatened? Will the walls of society come crumbling down if we recognise the equal right of all to marry? Is the breakdown of relationships and child abuse limited to lesbians and gay men?*

So many questions and very few rational answers from those seeking to maintain the *status quo*. Yet we have the support of enlightened souls such as Archbishop Desmond Tutu:

> "Rejecting gays and lesbians as the children of God must be nearly the ultimate blasphemy."

The first prize of our lobby is an amendment to the existing Marriage Act to recognise same-sex marriage in one law, rather than having a separate law for same-sex marriages. In the end, the Government proposes and manages to pass a clever compromise – a separate Civil Union Act open to all people wishing to join in a *marriage* or *civil partnership*. Heterosexual people can thus choose to marry under the old Marriage Act or under the new Act, but as same-sex couples we can only marry under the new Act.

Second prize perhaps, but significant progress in making South Africa only the sixth country in the world to recognise same-sex marriage in one form or another. And a sense of personal satisfaction – I feel I've come full circle from our advocacy and lobbying in the 1980s and 1990s before the inclusion of sexual orientation in our new Constitution.

There is lots of hype and public dialogue in the mass media following the Act's passing. The BBC's *World have your say* radio show debates current issues, with callers phoning in from around the globe. Local organisations ask Andile and me to go on the show to be interviewed and answer questions on how it feels to be able to be married officially. How can we say 'no' for the good of the cause? With a touch of nerves, we manage to pull it off better than we imagined we could at such short notice.

The joys of working through the Department of Home Affairs to solemnise civil unions (Zapiro, Independent Newspapers, 21 September 2006).

56. Partners A and B

"This thing is still new."

After thinking about our own position while on holiday, Andile and I decide in January 2007 to take steps to legalise our union. We have been a little put off by press reports of the Department of Home Affairs not being ready to implement the new Act due to capacity problems and the need to train staff on the new legislation. Little do we know what awaits us.

I begin the long journey of finding out what we need to do to get married under the Civil Union Act. I phone the Department of Home Affairs office in Cape Town. After several hours, I get through and am told there is a waiting list until the end of May. They suggest I phone the Wynberg office but should be aware that "they are very busy there".

Well, now I know. A day and a half later I finally get through to the Wynberg office:

> "You must come in personally with your IDs to get a marriage date appointment."

The next day I'm there. Fortunately, I've taken the morning off work. The Home Affairs website still lists an out-of-date physical address for the Wynberg office. I go there. Can you believe it – it's the address of SureSlim now, the place where Andile worked when we met! A board refers me to the new address in Wynberg that Home Affairs moved to over four years ago. This proves to be a sign of things to come.

The building is seething with people. There is a long queue waiting for 'Marriages and Deaths'. Marriages, I think, as I view the little man/woman icons depicting marriage:

I wonder if this is for us. I don't see any boy/boy or girl/girl icons. Has Home Affairs adapted its processes to reflect the new law?

After an hour or so of waiting, I should feel comforted. We are seated. Those waiting for IDs are less fortunate and seem to be in a two-to-three hour snake-like queue.

Eventually, I'm shouted in with a "next" to an oddly-shaped open-plan office with two officials in attendance. My official is busy on the phone. She puts the phone down and continues scribbling. I wait patiently. The phone rings. And rings. No one picks up. Now I can see why I waited a day and a half to get through to the office.

Summoning up oodles of patience and charm, I announce my purpose and hand over our IDs. I'm greeted with:

> "Which one is Partner A and which one is Partner B?"

I'm a bit thrown, but vaguely recall the wording of the marriage solemnisation in the Act referring impersonally to partners by letter:

"We don't really mind. I'm happy for you to choose."

I end up as Partner A and Andile as Partner B – maybe because my ID was on top? She scribbles hurriedly in her calendar diary and on a battered piece of paper. She rips it down the middle skewly, giving me one half and announcing:

"10h30 on Wednesday, 11 April, and don't be late. Now go to the photo section and make copies of your IDs and come back to me."

No explanation of the process. Or asking if I have any questions, or maybe if the date is suitable:

Communication skills are clearly not the strong suit in this office. What training did Home Affairs staff get for all those months? Was it maybe on procedural aspects of ascertaining who is A and who is B?

The slapdash bit of paper seems to be a stick-and-paste number from previous Marriage Act procedures. The language indicates it may have been translated from an Afrikaans original, such as the odd heading "Requirements which should be available on the day of marriage". This refers to the ID documents "of both bride and groom". Hello? Should this not be adapted to embrace and include same-sex couples? And then it lists the rules for our marriage day:

"No eating/drinking allowed in the building. No conveti/streamers allowed."

On my return with photocopies in hand, I have the audacity to ask the increasingly fidgety official:

"It says '2 photos (one per partner)'. Does that mean two pictures each? And should they be colour or black-and-white? Passport-size?"

She responds:

"Yes, two each. Colour or black-and-white. And size doesn't matter."

I throw my last curved ball:

"On the day, do we get a marriage certificate?"

"No, you'll get a handwritten one. The computerised one will come from Pretoria later."

I ask how long this will take:

"I don't know. This thing is still new."

Thank God, this 'thing' is over for now.

At least I came into this with some information, based on my background of involvement in advocacy and lobbying. Imagine:

> *How would I feel if I'd known nothing? How would Andile and I feel if we hadn't had our real marriage on our 2004 Commitment Day already and if this was to be our big day?*

Some people have reported Home Affairs officials turning applicants away and being homophobic at various offices. The official I saw didn't feel homophobic or disapproving. Just uncaring and not particularly interested in what she was doing. A sensitisation and communication skills training opportunity here? Subsequent events confirm that Home Affairs is in need of a serious overhaul and an injection of fresh capacity on all fronts, not just in the marriage division.

57. Very hot off the press

It's an opportunity to integrate my sexuality and living with HIV.

Triangle Project booklet, 2006 (photo by Kelly Walsh and design by Daniele Michelini).

...involved...reaching fruition...2007. Delayed, stretched out...ally on schedule, they've happened or ...about to! One of the joys of being a freelancer is that you have very little control over timelines and have to be prepared to negotiate unexpected changes of plan.

Triangle Project's new *HIV and sexuality* series has been a fulfilling challenge and has literally opened up new vistas. Working with Karen as a writer and Vista as Triangle's media co-ordinator, we have shaped four exciting booklets focusing on HIV testing, living positively with HIV, and sexuality and HIV – one for women and one for men.

The series aims to serve the needs of the lesbian and gay community, especially since we are so often invisible in the bulk of HIV/AIDS educational media. It's an opportunity to integrate two branches of my soul – my sexuality and living with HIV – as I write and develop the positive living booklet *Life is for living*.

The booklet includes quotes from old and new friends living positively with HIV. I hope users of the booklet will be as moved as I've been in sharing and learning from others. Interviewing has been a kind of two-way counselling. Our stories as people living with HIV have shaped my writing:

"Knowledge is power, so find out more about HIV and empower yourself. Strengthen your body, mind and soul to control your HIV – don't let it rule you. Try to use your deeper wisdom, sensitivity and experience of living with HIV to educate, help and support other people."

I try to use my sensitivity of living with HIV in editing Karen's three booklets that are packed with vital information. We want our readers to be more informed in the choices they make, and to share their awareness with others, as well as to live positively and openly with HIV when they feel comfortable.

The project is groundbreaking in embracing the GIPA Principle – people living with HIV participate actively by being interviewed and workshopping drafts of the booklets. Andile and I share our stories. We also have lots of fun doing a photo shoot with our Kommetjie space as location. There are private shoots within a shoot. Our guestroom hosts a seductive 'play safe, use condoms' scene for boys. And then our bath bubbles with the naughty smiles of girls at play!

The booklets promote the visibility of people living

with HIV, so interviewees who feel okay to be open participate together with models to ensure balance and representivity (gender- and rainbow-wise).

•••

A special edition of the AIDS Legal Network's *ALQ* newsletter on HIV prevention creates space for me to write *HIV prevention and treatment – the power of positive language*. I adapt and apply our Openly Positive positive language guidelines, while sharing my story:

> "Today I live positively and healthily with HIV. The double stigma of being gay and living with HIV has made my journey a sometimes bumpy and eventful one. How does language and being seen as different impact on our attitudes and actions around HIV prevention and treatment?"

I analyse the *power of language* and show how the stigmatising stain of HIV language has been part of mainstream media and our indigenous languages. I suggest that there is a way to turn the tide against the *language of power* that has negatively influenced South Africa's HIV/AIDS landscape in recent times. For example, ex-Deputy President Jacob Zuma explained in his rape trial how he took a shower after unprotected sex to minimise the possibility of HIV infection. I close by calling on readers to join me on a positive living journey:

> "I invite you to join me on a journey to help break down stigma, and in the spirit of positive language, to build an environment where people living with HIV can live open, visible, healthy and fulfilling lives."

•••

A two-year process of plain language editing work for the AIDS Law Project (ALP) culminates in the publishing of *Health and Democracy – A guide to human rights, law and policy in a post-apartheid South Africa*. The book powerfully captures 12 years of creative advocacy and litigation in developing access to health care in a democratic South Africa. I'm feeling a little elated. Unlike my unhappy toolkit experience, writers freely express the committed efforts of the TAC, ALP and others in advancing people's health rights in South Africa.

I travel to Joburg in February 2007 to celebrate the launch at Constitution Hill. It's my first chance to wander around the more people-friendly Constitutional Court and surrounding Old Fort Prison area. The artwork, influenced by Judge Albie Sachs, is a refreshing indicator of our burgeoning constitutional democracy.

With her foreword to the book and keynote address at its launch, Deputy Minister of Health, Nozizwe Madlala-Routledge, symbolises a change of tune from the Government towards the possibility of a real joint partnership with civil society on HIV/AIDS initiatives. The most telling moment is during ex-Judge Johann Kriegler's welcoming words to the Deputy Minister:

> "While we wish Minister Tshabalala-Msimang well in her recuperation from illness, we do wish *you* were the Minister!"

And so did the distinguished audience of human rights activists and academics. There is a spontaneous wave of nervous, hopeful smiles, punctuated with enthusiastic support. Wouldn't it be nice to say "Yes, Minister" to a Minister with the stature, commitment and political will to lead us in a positive, united direction?

•••

There is also the joy of my plain language editing efforts in helping to complete the second edition of the Community Law Centre's *Socio-Economic Rights in South Africa* resource book. It's the result of an 18-month process of dedicated team work that will be launched at the University of the Western Cape to coincide with the 10th anniversary of the Centre's Socio-Economic Rights Project in April 2007.

The book tries to bring together and share the many gains, achievements and ongoing challenges arising out of trying to turn the promise of the social and economic rights in our new Constitution into a lived reality for many more people in South Africa. We celebrate with partners and colleagues over a *sushi* supper. I'm happy to share a passion for Japanese food with the content editor Sibonile and production manager Fiona.

The toolkit is finally published: Tool 3 authored by me (design by Angela Tuck).

58. A time of closing and opening

It's the beginning of new life without parents and hopefully the end of an era of high conflict in the political landscape.

The never-ending rush of Kommetjie's waters is my constant companion. My life has a natural flow. As passages of our lives ebb, so new streams open up. The year of losing Dad has been a hard one, but one also punctuated with a few achievements and possibilities.

A 'back to the islands' break at the end of 2006 gives Andile and me the chance to rest and nourish our souls:

> *In a poignant flashback to a trip to Mauritius in the early 1970s with my Mom and brother, I'm conscious of having lost both my parents. I have a powerful memory of attraction to bronzed Creole men in those awakening, pubescent years.*

Now in my living dream, we first spend a memorable week in the Seychelles. There's the thrill of our first sandy, palm-fringed walk and frolicking in the warm Indian Ocean. Strange to think that nearby Muizenberg and all of the sizzling Seychelles share the same waters. Humidity levels are high as we float between tempting cocktails and sumptuous seafood. I'm lost in thoughts of Mom passionately collecting shells on the beach: lots of little 'specials' as Mom and Aunt Lucy would have called them.

My Mauritian return heralds the start of 2007. The glorious seven-coloured volcanic earth and bustling open-air markets have not changed. Our seaside hotel can't quite get its head around a boy-boy couple: "Are you sure you want a double bed?" they ask, after giving us two singles pushed together. And our New Year's Eve dinner menu is quaintly labelled "Mr and Mrs Gidana". No *Auld lang syne* at midnight here. Instead an extraordinarily loud and wildly colourful fireworks display!

Our year is off with a bang as we return to southern shores. It's a Misty Cliffs welcome. We eat leisurely with David and Mags at their seaside space, reminiscing about recent travels over wine, delicate tuna and veggies. It is the breathtaking Misty Cliffs panorama that inspired me to buy in Kommetjie when attending a house-warming party here about seven years before.

Andile is excited to begin a new school monitoring contract with Deloitte. I drift gently back into my usual mix of plain language and HIV consultancy work. With family, we are more focused on planning for Dad's consecration on 25 February. It's hard to believe it will be a year on 6 March. It's been so odd going to cricket at Newlands without Dad. I know I'm going to miss his entertaining snorts, comments and air punching during the Cricket World Cup.

The night before Dad's consecration, I gather my thoughts listening to and watching a DVD of Vladimir Horowitz's return concert to Russia in 1996 after an absence of 61 years. How Dad would have appreciated his momentous artistry and sense of occasion.

We have tried to capture a little of what Dad meant to us in his tombstone epitaph:

"In loving memory of Azriel Fine

20 June 1921 – 6 March 2006

Deeply mourned by Josephine, Andrea, Nicholas, Derrick, partners, grandchildren, family and friends.

Your energy, love, warmth and generosity will be with us forever."

Dad reserved his resting-place next to Mom. I feel a sense of resigned finality seeing their graves and tombstones alongside one another. My mind wanders often during the consecration and the get-together lunch hosted by Josephine.

My mood flows naturally to the next day when Andile and I savour the harmonious sounds of Il Divo at the Kirstenbosch Botanical Gardens. Dad's very much there, floating to the accompaniment of *My way*. We will honour his love of the outdoors by erecting a memorial bench or bridge at Kirstenbosch – a place to pause and remember, and to pursue renewed life as he would have wished.

Personally, it's the end of an era and the beginning of new life without parents. In the broader political landscape, an era of high conflict and contestation is hopefully ending too, or at least diminishing. There is a much stronger civil society participation in drawing up the new *HIV & AIDS and STI National Strategic Plan for South Africa 2007–2011*.

And, as if to complete a tortuous circle, the toolkit *To the other side of the mountain – the faces and voices of people living with HIV and AIDS in South Africa* is finally printed by the Department of Health:

Does it reflect the 'new mood', or is it just a case of a department under pressure to account for money spent and to produce resources before the end of another financial year?

It doesn't really matter why. To much relief, it's finally out, warts and all. A bit outdated and shorn of some of its critical elements, the bulk of its capacity-building and empowering contents are as valid now as they were when developed in 2003 for us as people living with HIV. Seeing the toolkit with its colourful faces and inspiring voices, I feel a sense of pride and sadness for the participants who are no longer with us. We can't bring back the time and lives we've lost, but we can redouble our efforts.

While the air is cleaner, all is not rosy. There'll be a need for continued and new struggles for improved treatment literacy, a speedier rollout of ARVs, and the national implementation of 'dual therapy' (Nevirapine and AZT) for pregnant moms living with HIV – to protect their babies from HIV infection.

And we'll have to push for the registration and use of Tenofovir, Truvada and other new medicines in the public sector. Also, the Government should urgently take a fresh look at sustaining social grants for people recovering while on ARVs, as well as extending grants to the many children heading households and becoming 'adults before their time'.

Celebrating our legal union at Rhodes Memorial with our witnesses MamLu and Basti.

59. My Unfinished Symphony

Testing HIV positive has taken me on an eight-year journey to a life-affirming identity of living, and loving and being loved, with HIV as one part of who I am.

Lift-off! I feel a little lighter without the toolkit cloud hanging over me. With my own resources and the precious support of my nearest and dearest, I have reached the other side of my own mountain.

Another momentous beacon awaits Andile and me as our 11 April marriage date nears. Bastienne and MamLu, in her retirement year in Cape Town, will be our witnesses. It feels unreal: no catering, tents and worrying about the weather as we did in December 2004. Yet it's water-blessing time again. The heavens open in a steady drizzle to cool the day that will make our union official.

Basti adorns us with sunflowers on our arrival at Home Affairs in Wynberg, a lovely link with the sunflowers that lit up our Commitment Day. We have to wait for half an hour or so beyond our 10h30 marriage appointment time. We are ushered in not with a welcome but rather by "witness IDs please".

We're doing our best to feel relaxed in the impersonal Home Affairs surrounds. The marriage room is bleak, decorated with a national flag, a bulging computer, some papers and a fingerprint inkpad. I introduce the four of us to the marriage officer by first name to break the ice. She warms a little, but is too caught up in to-and-fro paperwork to really engage with us as human beings:

"Do you Partner A declare that as far as you know there is no lawful impediment to your proposed civil union with Partner B here present and that you call all here present to witness that you take Partner B as your lawful spouse?"

We both 'do'. We kiss and are pronounced married. We have elected a *marriage* rather than a *civil partnership* under the new Civil Union Act. We receive a temporary *Abridged Civil Union Registration Certificate* and we will wait a month or two to apply, pay for and collect our permanent marriage certificate once we are registered in Pretoria.

We've done it! It still hasn't quite sunk in while we enjoy chocolate cake and tea with MamLu and Basti at Rhodes Memorial, back to where we lunched after Andile received news that he was living with HIV in 2003. The bridal couple meander to Uitsig wine estate for a peaceful, dozy champagne lunch. We will celebrate again with Elaine and Vita on Saturday night.

There's a continued sense of completing another circle in life. I reflect on our long struggle in reaching the moment allowing us to marry in law. I think of my secret meeting with Albie Sachs in London in the late 1980s when I was delegated to open doors to lobbying the ANC's Constitutional Committee in exile, en route to the historic achievement of having sexual orientation included in our 1996 new Constitution. Albie's words were wise and prophetic:

> "Don't push for marriage first. Go for equality, dignity and non-discrimination. Leave marriage till last."

Now I'm home at last with my man, my life partner, my spouse. We don't feel very different. Just relieved and kind of at peace.

Words and thoughts are flashing through my mind:

My Mom's "Are you happy?" during my university years.

"Mom, I've got something I've been wanting to share with you," when coming out to my Mom.

"I'm gay and I'm proud of it" to my Dad.

"Dad… I'm doing well health-wise. But I need you to know that I too have been living with HIV for a few years…"

Jogging on the sand, I'm 48 years young. I'm taking better care of myself than ever before and feeling happier than I've ever known. I still wish to feel the salty waters and sultry air of Cape Verde, the home of my musical granny, Cesária Évora. A future trip maybe.

Starting as a jarring wake-up call, testing HIV positive has taken me on an eight-year journey to a life-affirming identity of living, and loving and being loved, with HIV as one part of who I am.

Forward and onward to new balances, new challenges and new pleasures as I breathe in Kommetjie's air on another first day of the rest of my life. Martina Navratilova's words in a TV documentary echo for me now, with the harmonious backing chords of the sea:

> "Do what you love.
> Love what you do.
> The rest is detail."

In the absence of the Minister of Health, a new sense of working together – will it last? (Zapiro, Sunday Times, 18 March 2007).

Postscript

Our world of living with HIV is constantly changing. This postscript captures just a few things that have happened since I ended my story with legalising my marriage to Andile on 11 April 2007:

There's a step forward on treatment when Tenofovir and Truvada are finally registered for use in South Africa in May 2007. No more section 21 applications to the MCC for me, but still we will have to advocate for the Government to get these new medicines at a lower price for public sector use.

We continue to lose brave fighters for our rights as people living with HIV. Early in May, we hear the very sad news that Lungi Mazibuko, campaigner for the Western Cape Networking AIDS Community of South Africa (NACOSA) and so many causes, has passed on after developing multi-drug resistant TB. Andile and I write a message for her memorial service:

Lungi, you will live on in our hearts as a special, unique person.
You fought for us as people living with HIV.
You spoke out for lesbians and gay men.
You were in the trenches for all women.
You beamed. You inspired. You were selfless.

We wish you were able to take the ARVs you needed when there was still time.
We needed you for so much longer!
Hamba kahle, dear Lungi.

With much expectation, I head off to Home Affairs in the middle of May to collect our marriage certificate. Three queues and four hours later, I am deflated. They have managed to mess up our certificate: instead of registering our union as a *marriage*, they have registered it as a *civil partnership*, even though we clearly chose marriage during our April ceremony. The supervisor assures us it is a "human error" and the certificate is sent back to Pretoria to be corrected and re-issued. We now have the correct version after an eventful journey.

The mood at the South African AIDS Conference in Durban at the start of June is thankfully different. Under the stewardship of a restructured South African National AIDS Council (SANAC) headed by Deputy President Phumzile Mlambo-Ngcuka, there is a real sense that, at last, the Government and civil society will be able to work together towards the Conference theme of *Building Consensus on Prevention, Treatment and Care*.

The *Conference Declaration* guides action towards implementing the new National Strategic Plan (NSP), with the Preamble recognising:

> "The need for active participation of people living with HIV and AIDS in implementing and monitoring the NSP."

I am feeling energised and glad to be part of follow-up efforts to organise our sector of people living with HIV to be active participants in the joint efforts that lie ahead of us. We are collectively ready to assist with dramatically upscaling HIV counselling and testing towards everyone knowing their HIV status and being able to take responsible steps to stay healthy.

The middle of June sees me begin my new Truvada combination of tablets, together with my regular Stocrin. Truvada combines FTC, a sister drug of 3TC, and Tenofovir in one tablet, meaning that I'm now down to a much more manageable two tablets once a day. My medicines are doing a great job and I'm coping well.

The only 'side effect' I see nowadays when I look in the mirror are tinges of white: it's not shaving cream, but my maturing grey edges. I'll simply have to accept that I'm nearing my half-century in 2008. At least I'll be 50 not out!

As we near the time for registering Openly Positive as a non-profit trust, there's a real sense of coming home when Anne and Andile, the midwives who helped Elaine and me give birth to the Openly Positive idea in 2004, join us as trustees of The Openly Positive Trust.

June 2007

Lessons and questions for discussion

"To love oneself is the beginning of a lifelong romance."

Oscar Wilde

On pages 213–221 we summarise some of the things I have learnt in my journey of living with HIV. The questions encourage you to think about what these lessons mean for you in your own situation, and to work out your own way of responding to HIV and other challenges in your life.

You may wish to use these lessons and questions on your own, in workshops or in support group discussions. When you do this, you are welcome to photocopy these *Lessons and questions for discussion* pages. You can also add your own lessons and questions in the empty spaces.

These issues may be difficult to think about or deal with – on page 222 is a list of some organisations you can contact for further help.

STIGMA, DENIAL, SILENCE AND DISCRIMINATION

Lessons

- After testing HIV positive, my first step to reducing stigma was to accept inside myself that I am living with HIV – I had to overcome my inner voice of denial and say: "This is real and it's happening to me."

- HIV is not a badge of shame – when we live with HIV, it is one part of who we are and one part of our lives.

- Once you stop blaming the past and start accepting your HIV status, you will be much more able to look after yourself and to support others.

- When you feel stronger, you can link up with other people living with HIV and speak out openly to challenge stigma and discrimination. For example, you could challenge a newspaper that labels us "HIV sufferers".

Questions

- Why are stigma, denial and discrimination around HIV/AIDS still so strong in South Africa?

- What can we do to get people talking more openly and to reduce stigma and discrimination around HIV/AIDS? For example, does it help to use positive, sensitive language in speaking and writing about HIV/AIDS?

- In what ways have you tried to break the silence around HIV and living with HIV?

Clouds move: Lessons and questions for discussion, © Derrick Fine 2007

HIV TESTING

Lessons

- I delayed having an HIV test because of stigma, fear and focusing on my work and relationship issues, instead of putting myself first.

- Finding out your HIV status is the first step to taking care of yourself – staying HIV negative if you test HIV negative, and living healthily and getting the care, support and treatment you need if you test HIV positive.

- Knowing your HIV status is an insurance policy for your future and the future of the people you love.

Questions

- Have you had an HIV test?

- What is stopping you from having an HIV test? Have you thought about getting advice and counselling to encourage you to test?

- Do you regularly retest for HIV if you are HIV negative, yet sexually active?

Clouds move: Lessons and questions for discussion, © Derrick Fine 2007

SAFER SEX

Lessons

- I felt so much better about myself when I was able to disclose I was living with HIV to my partner, before anything intimate happened between us.

- Having unsafe sex does not bring trust in a relationship – trust is about loving someone enough to want to protect them.

- Having safer sex, for example, using a condom, is not about being promiscuous – it's about being responsible and trying to prevent HIV transmission or re-infection.

Questions

- What do we mean by *safer sex*?

- Do you practise safer sex all the time? If not, what stops you?

- What is the best way of negotiating safer sex, for example, with a regular partner or with a partner outside of a committed relationship?

DISCLOSING, GETTING SUPPORT AND EDUCATING OTHERS

Lessons

- Starting to disclose that I am living with HIV helped to take a big weight off my shoulders – I realised I don't have to carry it alone.

- Take it one step at a time, beginning with disclosing to one person who you trust, for example, another person who is openly living with HIV.

- Disclosing is like dropping a stone in a pond – one disclosure gives you the strength to disclose to more people when you are ready.

- Don't rush a disclosure – for each disclosure, find a good time and a quiet place that feels right for you, and follow up to see how the person you have disclosed to is feeling afterwards.

- Disclosing is an ongoing process of receiving support, giving support to others around HIV and other challenges in their lives, and educating family, friends and work colleagues about HIV and AIDS.

Questions

- If you have been unable to disclose that you are living with HIV, what is holding you back?

- What has been your experience of disclosing, for example, to a partner, to a child or to a parent?

- How has disclosing helped you, and what tips can you suggest to make disclosing easier for others?

- What are the best ways to educate others about HIV and AIDS to make them more aware before and after you disclose to them?

Clouds move: Lessons and questions for discussion, © Derrick Fine 2007

COMING OUT ABOUT YOUR SEXUAL ORIENTATION

Lessons

- It is okay to be different, for example, to be gay – the most important thing was to accept who I am and to be myself.

- Choose one trusted person to talk to first, for example, a friend, a family member, a counsellor or someone else who is openly lesbian/gay.

- Take it one step at a time and at your own pace – you don't have to tell everyone at once.

- Social and legal recognition of same-sex unions encourages people to have committed, loving relationships.

Questions

- Has it been difficult for you to talk about your sexuality and to come out, for example, at home or at school?

- How did you feel once you started the process of coming out to one or two close people?

- How can you help someone who you know is struggling to be open about his/her sexual orientation?

- How can you help create greater tolerance and acceptance of difference and diversity in South Africa, for example, the equal right of everyone to dignity and to marry?

Clouds move: Lessons and questions for discussion, © Derrick Fine 2007

TAKING ANTIRETROVIRALS

Lessons

- I went onto ARVs in the private sector when my CD4 count dropped to 300 instead of waiting until my count was 200 to qualify in the public sector – I wanted to take control of my body and my life.

- In the public sector, you can qualify for ARVs if your CD4 count is over 200 and you are experiencing opportunistic infections like TB or pneumonia.

- I never miss a dose of my ARVs – I think of them as if they are my daily dose of vitamins.

- Try to get as much information as you can about ARVs and other medication for treating infections by asking, reading and attending treatment literacy workshops – the more you know, the better prepared you will be for when you need to take ARVs or other medication.

Questions

- After testing HIV positive, did you have counselling to help keep you strong mentally and have you had regular check-ups to monitor your CD4 count?

- Have you considered starting to take ARVs if your CD4 count is under 200 or you are experiencing opportunistic infections?

- How are you coping on ARVs? Have you spoken to others coping well with ARVs to get advice on how to cope better, for example, monitoring your viral load and keeping an eye on drug side effects and resistance?

- How can we ensure that people taking ARVs in the public sector have access to more affordable drug options when experiencing side effects or resistance to some drugs?

Clouds move: Lessons and questions for discussion, © Derrick Fine 2007

VISIBILITY AND PARTICIPATION AS PEOPLE LIVING WITH HIV

Lessons

- As people living with HIV and AIDS, we need to make sure that our faces are seen and our voices are heard – we need to speak up for ourselves.

- "Nothing about us without us" – we can use our experience of living with HIV to help guide policies and programmes, and make them more sensitive and effective in dealing with the issues that affect us.

- Our greater visibility will help to reduce stigma and build a culture of consulting us as people living with HIV, based on our democracy and the values in our South African Constitution.

Questions

- What does the *GIPA Principle* mean to you (the idea that, as people living with HIV, we should participate in policies, issues and programmes that affect us)?

- What stops you from being able to link up with other people living with HIV to make sure that our voices are heard?

- How can we ensure that we stand together as people living with HIV to participate more effectively in things that affect us?

Clouds move: Lessons and questions for discussion, © Derrick Fine 2007

FACING THE FUTURE WITH HOPE

Lessons

- Today is the first day of the rest of my life – and I will do everything I can to make sure it's a healthy, stress-free, long, fulfilling life.

- With access to ARV treatment, HIV is a manageable condition if you live positively and take care of yourself, for example, adhere to your treatment, eat healthily and exercise regularly.

- Loving and being loved is a powerful medicine in reducing stress, worries, aches and pains.

Questions

- What does the idea of *positive living* mean to you?

- What is your recipe for having hope in the future while living with HIV?

- How can knowing your HIV status help you to plan a better future for you and your loved ones?

Clouds move: Lessons and questions for discussion, © Derrick Fine 2007

Examples of South African contacts for help, advice, counselling, support, treatment and public education

- AIDS Helpline (National Department of Health): 0800 012 322 + www.doh.gov.za

- AIDS Law Project: 011 356 4100 + www.alp.org.za

- AIDS Legal Network: 021 447 8435 + www.aln.org.za

- Centre for the Study of AIDS: 012 420 4395 + www.csa.za.org

- Community Health Media Trust: 021 788 9163 + www.beatit.co.za

- Durban Lesbian and Gay Community and Health Centre: 031 301 2145 + www.gaycentre.org.za

- OUT Lesbian, Gay, Bisexual, Transgender Well-being: 012 344 5108 + www.out.org.za

- Treatment Action Campaign: 021 788 3507 + www.tac.org.za

- Triangle Project: 021 448 3812 + www.triangle.org.za
  (services and safe spaces for lesbian, gay, bisexual and transgender people)

Clouds move: Lessons and questions for discussion, © Derrick Fine 2007

Positive language guidelines for HIV/AIDS communication

"I will remember that I don't help patients, I help people."

The Link Pharmacist's Oath

These are Openly Positive's positive language guidelines to encourage the use of more sensitive, non-stigmatising language when writing and talking about HIV/AIDS in our lives. The 12 guidelines suggest ways of turning negative, stigmatising language into positive, more people-friendly language.

You are welcome to photocopy these *Positive language guidelines* pages for use on your own, in workshops or in support groups.

Guideline 1:

Avoid labelling people or reducing ourselves to our HIV status alone

Recognise HIV as one part of who we are

NEGATIVE LANGUAGE	POSITIVE LANGUAGE
HIV positive person or *HIV-infected person*	*Person living with HIV* or *person who has HIV*

Clouds move: Positive language guidelines, © The Openly Positive Trust 2007

Guideline 2:

Don't disempower	Try to empower and give hope
NEGATIVE LANGUAGE *AIDS victims*	**POSITIVE LANGUAGE** *People facing the challenges of living with HIV and AIDS* or *people affected by HIV and AIDS*

Guideline 3:

Don't stigmatise or judge	Humanise
NEGATIVE LANGUAGE *AIDS orphans*	**POSITIVE LANGUAGE** *Children orphaned by AIDS* or *children affected by AIDS*

Clouds move: Positive language guidelines, © The Openly Positive Trust 2007

Guideline 4:

Don't victimise or criminalise	Humanise
NEGATIVE LANGUAGE *HIV sufferers* or *AIDS carriers*	**POSITIVE LANGUAGE** *People living with HIV*

Guideline 5:

Don't sensationalise	Contextualise, describe and inform
NEGATIVE LANGUAGE *Full-blown AIDS*	**POSITIVE LANGUAGE** *AIDS* (and explain HIV progression, as there is no *half-blown AIDS*)
NEGATIVE LANGUAGE *The AIDS disaster* or *the AIDS time bomb*	**POSITIVE LANGUAGE** *The AIDS epidemic* or *HIV progression* (with ARV treatment, progression to AIDS is no longer inevitable)

Clouds move: Positive language guidelines, © The Openly Positive Trust 2007

Guideline 6:

Don't depersonalise and create distance	Personalise and identify with people
NEGATIVE LANGUAGE *Patient*	**POSITIVE LANGUAGE** *Person, Elaine, Derrick*
NEGATIVE LANGUAGE *Research cohort*	**POSITIVE LANGUAGE** *Research participant*

Guideline 7:

Don't generalise or be vague	Specify and be precise
NEGATIVE LANGUAGE *AIDS transmission* or *AIDS test*	**POSITIVE LANGUAGE** *HIV transmission* or *HIV test* (you can't pass on AIDS or have an AIDS test)
NEGATIVE LANGUAGE *AIDS virus*	**POSITIVE LANGUAGE** *HIV* (there is no such thing as the AIDS virus – rather say HIV is the virus that causes AIDS if you need to explain)

Clouds move: Positive language guidelines, © The Openly Positive Trust 2007

Guideline 8:

Don't generalise with individual people

NEGATIVE LANGUAGE

She is living with HIV/AIDS

Try to individualise with people

POSITIVE LANGUAGE

She is living with HIV or *She is living with AIDS*
(if factually correct and she has consented)

Guideline 9:

Try not to disguise or avoid

NEGATIVE LANGUAGE

The virus

Be as open and transparent as possible

POSITIVE LANGUAGE

HIV

NEGATIVE LANGUAGE

He died after a long illness

POSITIVE LANGUAGE

He died from AIDS-related TB

Clouds move: Positive language guidelines, © The Openly Positive Trust 2007

Guideline 10:

Don't exclude | **Be inclusive**

NEGATIVE LANGUAGE

AIDS conference or *AIDS policy*

POSITIVE LANGUAGE

HIV/AIDS conference or *HIV/AIDS policy* (for convenience, we use *HIV/AIDS* to describe things like policies, conferences, committees, programmes and work, but with people we rather use *HIV and AIDS*)

Guideline 11:

Avoid unnecessary abbreviations | **Use abbreviations selectively and sensitively**

NEGATIVE LANGUAGE

PLHAs (in a speech)

POSITIVE LANGUAGE

People living with HIV and AIDS (more people-friendly, although an abbreviation may be better with repeated use in a long written document)

Clouds move: Positive language guidelines, © The Openly Positive Trust 2007

Guideline 12:

Don't confuse or be inconsistent | Be clear and consistent in one document, and make sure headlines and captions to photographs are sensitive and consistent

NEGATIVE LANGUAGE	POSITIVE LANGUAGE
AIDS patients and *people on ARV treatment* (in one paragraph)	*People on ARV treatment* (rather use one people-friendly term)

Clouds move: Positive language guidelines, © The Openly Positive Trust 2007

Glossary

Adherence	When you are *adherent*, you always take the right dose of your medication at the correct time every day.
AIDS	Acquired Immune Deficiency Syndrome – the final possible stage of HIV progression.
ALP	AIDS Law Project.
ANC	African National Congress.
ARVs	Antiretroviral drugs – anti-HIV drugs to reduce the amount of HIV in your body and strengthen your immune system.
AZT	Azido-thymidine, otherwise known as Zidovudine (trade name *Retrovir*), an ARV used in ARV combinations of three drugs and now also recommended, together with Nevirapine, in preventing mother-to-child HIV transmission.
B&B	Bed and breakfast accommodation.
BBC	British Broadcasting Corporation.
Bésame mucho	*Kiss me lots* – the Spanish title of a song by Cesária Évora.
Boetie	Brother or little brother, a term of endearment, in Afrikaans.
Bouillabaisse	French-style fish soup.
Bra	Brother, in South African slang.
Businyanga	Honeymoon – a coined word, from the isiXhosa words *ubusi* (honey) and *inyanga* (moon).

CD4 count	A measure of the strength of your immune system that counts the number of CD4 cells in each cubic millimetre of blood. *CD4* is a protein on the surface of some cells onto which HIV can bind. The higher the number of CD4 cells you have, the stronger your immune system is.
Combivir	The ARV combination of AZT and 3TC.
Coming out	The process of being open about your sexual orientation, for example, when you come out as lesbian or gay.
Denial	When we refuse to accept something – *denialism* refers to the disturbing trend of some senior political leaders and others in South Africa, who refuse to accept the reality that HIV exists and, if untreated, can progress to AIDS.
d4T	Stavudine (trade name *Zerit*), an ARV.
Disclosing/Disclosure	The process of starting to share with others that you are living with HIV.
Discrimination	Being treated differently, usually in an unfair way, for example, the stigma around HIV can lead to discrimination, such as being unfairly treated or dismissed at work.
Ekhaya	At home, in isiXhosa.
Fado	Portuguese music that is similar to Cape Verdean *morna* with its mood of longing and missing dear ones.
Family	Broader use of the word *family* to mean someone who is also lesbian, gay or bisexual.
FTC	Emtricitabine (trade name *Emtriva*), an ARV.
GIPA Principle	The Greater Involvement of People Living with HIV and AIDS (GIPA) Principle is an initiative of the United Nations to ensure the active participation of people living with HIV in policies, issues and programmes affecting us.

GNP+	Global Network of People Living with HIV and AIDS.
HIV	Human Immunodeficiency Virus – the virus that weakens your immune system and can lead to AIDS if not properly treated.
Home Affairs	Department of Home Affairs, South Africa.
Homophobic	Showing an irrational fear of, or not wanting to associate with, lesbians and gay men.
ID	Identity Document.
Iindlovu	Elephants, in isiXhosa.
Joburg	Short for Johannesburg.
KCHR	Karoo Centre for Human Rights, Beaufort West, Western Cape, South Africa.
Klawerjas	A card game.
LEAP	The Legal Education Action Project at the Institute of Criminology, University of Cape Town, during the 1980s and 1990s.
Lekker	Nice or tasty, in Afrikaans.
LGBT	Lesbian, gay, bisexual or transgender.
Mama	Mother, also used as a term of respect, in isiXhosa.
MCC	Medicines Control Council, South Africa.
MoH	Ministry of Health, South Africa.
Morna	A style of Cape Verdean music that captures a sense of longing for loved ones and home.

NAPWA	National Association of People Living with HIV and AIDS, South Africa.
NDoH	National Department of Health, South Africa.
NEMATO	Nelson Mandela Township, Port Alfred, Eastern Cape, South Africa.
Nevirapine	An ARV used to prevent mother-to-child HIV transmission and in ongoing ARV combinations of three drugs.
NGO	Non-governmental organisation.
Non-stigmatising	Talking about HIV/AIDS in a way that does not negatively label people living with or affected by HIV and AIDS.
NSP	National Strategic Plan – South Africa's HIV/AIDS and Sexually Transmitted Infections National Strategic Plan 2007–2011.
Opportunistic infection	A specific infection that causes illness when your immune system is damaged by HIV, for example, TB, pneumonia or cryptococcal meningitis. It is called *opportunistic* because it takes advantage of the opportunity created by your weaker immune system.
Out	To *out* someone is to reveal that the person is lesbian, gay or bisexual.
PLHA	Abbreviation sometimes used for people living with HIV and AIDS.
Positive language	Using positive, non-stigmatising language to talk about ourselves as people living and surviving with HIV.
Positive living	Having a positive outlook and approach to life, love and health, including living positively and openly with HIV.
Regimen	Combination of drugs, for example, ARV regimens usually have three drugs that must be taken together.

Resistance	When an ARV drug stops working effectively because the drug is unable to stop some of the HIV in your blood from reproducing. Your viral load is then likely to increase and you may have to change to a different ARV combination.
SABC	South African Broadcasting Corporation.
Savanna	A popular South African cider drink.
SDU	Schools Development Unit, University of Cape Town.
Side effects	As with all medicines, different ARVs have their own side effects, for example, fat redistribution or wasting. If side effects continue for a long time or are severe, you will need to change your ARV combination.
Stigma	When you think about yourself in a negative way, or others have negative attitudes and feelings towards you as someone living with HIV, or facing another challenge like living with disability or being gay.
STIs	Sexually transmitted infections.
Stocrin	Efavirenz (trade name *Sustiva*), an ARV.
TAC	Treatment Action Campaign, South Africa.
Tamatiebredie	Traditional Cape-style meat stew in a tomato-based sauce.
TB	Tuberculosis.
Tenofovir	Viread (trade name *Tenofovir disoproxil fumarate*), a more recent ARV with fewer side effects.
3TC	Lamivudine (trade name *Epivir*), an ARV.

Treatment literacy	Finding out as much as you can about HIV treatments, such as ARVs and medicines to treat opportunistic infections, for example, the different drugs, when you have to take them, possible side effects, and different doses for children.
Truvada	The ARV combination of FTC and Tenofovir.
Ubuntu	Being human – the spirit of looking out for each other in African culture (from a saying meaning 'a person is a person because of other people').
UCT	University of Cape Town.
Umbhaco	Traditional fabric, in isiXhosa.
UN	United Nations.
UNAIDS	Joint United Nations Programme on HIV/AIDS.
Undetectable	When your viral load is below 40 (previously 50) – the lowest level of detection in standard HIV laboratory tests – the amount of HIV is called 'undetectable', although it is still present in your body in small quantities.
UNDP	United Nations Development Programme.
Viral load	A measure of the amount of HIV in a sample of your blood. Your HIV viral load shows how HIV is reproducing in your body – the higher your viral load, the more HIV there is in your blood.
WOMAD	World of Music, Arts and Dance festival in England and other countries.

References and useful reading

We mention the website, if available, the first time we individually list an organisation or institution:

AIDS Law Project:
Booklet series on your HIV/AIDS-related rights to health care and your rights in the workplace (www.alp.org.za)

AIDS Law Project and AIDS Legal Network:
HIV/AIDS and the Law – a resource manual, 3rd edition, 2003

AIDS Law Project and Treatment Action Campaign:
HIV in our lives – a booklet of medical information sheets for people living with HIV, support groups and clinics, 2003

AIDS Legal Network:
ALQ quarterly newsletter, including information on prevention, treatment and living with HIV (www.aln.org.za)

Brand, Alan:
Positively Alive – a guide to inner healing while living with HIV and AIDS, 2005 (www.jacana.co.za)

Cameron, Edwin:
Witness to AIDS – a book by a judge sharing his life and work living with HIV and AIDS, with contributions by Nathan Geffen, 2005 (www.tafelberg.com)

Community Health Media Trust:
Siyayinqoba/Beat It! – weekly positive living TV programme on SABC1 (www.beatit.co.za)

Community Law Centre and Khoza, Sibonile (editor):
Socio-Economic Rights in South Africa – a resource book, 2nd edition, including a focus on health care rights and social security rights, 2007 (www.communitylawcentre.org.za)

Day Zero Film & Video for Social Transformation and Empowerment Projects:
Video collection and facilitator's guide (2002) to promote debate and discussion around HIV/AIDS-related topics such as disclosure, discrimination, treatment and living positively (www.steps.co.za)

Department of Health, South Africa:
Living Openly – stories by people living with HIV, 2000 (www.doh.gov.za)

Department of Health, South Africa, and the POLICY Project, South Africa:
To the other side of the mountain: The faces and voices of people living with HIV and AIDS in South Africa – a toolkit with stories and guidelines on disclosure, rights, and communication, facilitation and advocacy skills, 2005 (www.policyproject.com)

Fox, Jane:
Nkosi's story – a book about the life of Nkosi Johnson, the young HIV/AIDS activist, 2002 (www.lifestoryproject.com)

Global Network of People Living with HIV and AIDS (GNP+):
Positive Development – a manual on positive living, with information on support groups, advocacy and campaigning, 1998 (www.gnpplus.net)

Hassim, Adila; Heywood, Mark; and Berger, Jonathan (editors):
Health and Democracy – a guide to human rights, health law and policy in a post-apartheid South Africa, 2007 (www.siberink.co.za)

Health24:
Online support and information on many health issues, including diet, fitness, medical aid and mental health (www.health24.com)

International AIDS Society and GNP+:
Changing lives for 25 years and counting: HIV professionals living with HIV/AIDS – background paper for AIDS 2006 Conference, Toronto (www.iasociety.org)

Joint United Nations Programme on HIV/AIDS (UNAIDS):
Report on the global AIDS epidemic – a UNAIDS 10th anniversary special edition, 2006 (www.unaids.org)

Keita, Salif:
Moffou – poem December 2001, on *Moffou* album sleeve, 2002 (Universal Music)

Koch, Blaise:
In, around, through and out: an actor's life – a book about living with HIV as part of a rich life, 2002 (Spearhead – www.newafricabooks.co.za)

Levin, Adam:
Aidsafari – a book by a journalist about his journey of living with HIV and AIDS, 2005 (www.zebrapress.co.za)

McGregor, Liz

Khabzela: the life and times of a South African – a book about the life of Yfm DJ Fana Khaba, 2005 (www.jacana.co.za)

National AIDS Manual, United Kingdom:

Booklet series on a wide range of HIV/AIDS topics, including stigma, women, ARVs, TB, hepatitis, mental health and nutrition (www.aidsmap.com)

Nattrass, Nicoli:

Mortal combat: AIDS denialism and the struggle for antiretrovirals in South Africa, 2007 (www.ukznpress.co.za)

Nin, Khadja:

Ya – album dedication, 1998 (www.bmg.fr)

Openly Positive; Fine, Derrick; and Maane, Elaine:

Positive language in HIV/AIDS communication – guidelines on speaking and writing in positive, non-stigmatising language, 2005 (see page 223–229 of this book and www.openlypositive.com)

Orr, Neil:

Positive Health – a booklet, with lots of information on things like healthy eating, a healthy mind and a healthy soul, 2004 (Double Storey Books)

Oryema, Geoffrey:

Night to Night – album track *Dancing steps*, 1996 (Real World)

OUT LGBT Well-being:

Understanding the Challenges facing Gay and Lesbian South Africans – a booklet with some guidelines for service providers, 2007 (www.out.za.org)

Rasebotsa, Nobantu; Samuelson, Meg; and Thomas, Kylie (editors):

Nobody ever said AIDS – stories and poems from Southern Africa, 2004 (www.kwela.com)

Siffre, Labi:

So Strong – album track *Something inside so strong*, 1988 (China Records)

Sunday Times:

Everyone knows someone – special reports campaign with stories of people living with and affected by HIV and AIDS (www.sundaytimes.co.za)

Thomas, Stephanie and Coutsoudis, Anna:

Quality living with HIV – a toolkit for care providers, 2004 (Department of Paediatrics and Child Health, University of KwaZulu-Natal)

Treatment Action Campaign:
Equal Treatment magazine, with information on treatment, positive living and campaigning around rights for people living with HIV and AIDS (www.tac.org.za)

Treatment Action Campaign:
ARVs in our lives – a handbook for people living with HIV and treatment advocates in support groups, clinics and communities, 2006

Triangle Project:
Triangle News – quarterly newsletter, including information on HIV services and on support groups for the lesbian, gay, bisexual and transgender community (www.triangle.org.za)

Triangle Project; Fine, Derrick; and Smith, Charmaine:
Understanding sexual diversity in the classroom – Educators Awareness Project Workshop Manual, 2005

Triangle Project and Kraan, Karen:
Booklet series on sexual orientation – young people exploring sexuality; bisexuality; information for parents and guardians; and people exploring their sexuality at a mature age, 2005

Triangle Project; Kraan, Karen; and Fine, Derrick:
Booklet series on HIV and sexual health for the lesbian, gay, bisexual and transgender community – HIV testing; *Life is for living:* living positively with HIV; women, sexuality and HIV; and men, sexuality and HIV, 2006

Van Dijk, Lutz and Chubb, Karin (translation):
Crossing the Line – the fictional story of a young boy, a talented soccer player, who lives with and is affected by HIV and AIDS, 2006 (www.shuter.co.za)

Wilde, Oscar:
Quote from a selection by the Irish dramatist, novelist and poet, compiled by Rand Lindsly (www.quotationspage.com)